W9-BNZ-189

THE TEXT, CANON, AND PRINCIPAL VERSIONS OF THE BIBLE

THE TEXT, CANON, AND PRINCIPAL VERSIONS OF THE BIBLE

By

Elmer E. Flack, Bruce M. Metzger,

and others

A Brief Survey of Recent Research

Extracted from the

TWENTIETH CENTURY ENCYCLOPEDIA OF RELIGIOUS KNOWLEDGE

BAKER BOOK HOUSE

Grand Rapids 6, Michigan

1956

Library of Congress Catalog Card Number: 56-7580.

Copyright, 1956, by
BAKER BOOK HOUSE

PHOTOLITHOPRINTED BY CUSHING - MALLOY, INC.
ANN ARBOR, MICHIGAN, UNITED STATES OF AMERICA
1956

PREFACE

In the autumn of 1955 the Baker Book House published in two volumes the *Twentieth Century Encyclopedia of Religious Knowledge* under the general editorship of Professor Lefferts A. Loetscher of Princeton Theological Seminary. The aim of these volumes is sufficiently expressed in their sub-title, *An Extension of the New Schaff-Herzog Encyclopedia of Religious Knowledge.* Since the articles in the latter were in most cases completed at the beginning of the present century, the two supplementary volumes presuppose their solid scholarship and seek to carry the work forward for another half century.

In response to a suggestion made to the publisher, several articles bearing on the text, canon, and principal versions of the Bible have been selected from the *Twentieth Century Encyclopedia* and are now issued in this book. The sequence of the several contributions, with an indication in each case of authorship, may be seen by consulting the *Table of Contents.* The list of abbreviations on p. 8 is reprinted from the larger work.

The following will serve to identify the scholars whose work appears here:

Millar Burrows, Ph.D., Winkley Professor of Biblical Theology, Yale University.

David Diringer, Litt.D., University Lecturer in Semitic Epigraphy, University of Cambridge.

Elmer E. Flack, Th.D., D.D., LL.D., Dean and Professor of Exegetical Theology, Hamma Divinity School; Old Testament editor of the *Twentieth Century Encyclopedia of Religious Knowledge.*

Henry S. Gehman, Ph.D., S.T.D., Litt.D., Professor of Old Testament Literature and Chairman of the Department of Biblical Studies, Princeton Theological Seminary; Lecturer in Semitic Languages, Princeton University.

F. Wilbur Gingrich, Ph.D., Professor of Greek, Albright College.

Howard T. Kuist, Ph.D., Charles T. Haley Professor of Biblical Theology for the Teaching of English Bible, Princeton Theological Seminary.

Bruce M. Metzger, Ph.D., D.D., Professor of New Testament Language and Literature, Princeton Theological Seminary; New Testament Editor of the *Twentieth Century Encyclopedia of Religious Knowledge.*

Eugene A. Nida, Ph.D., Secretary of Translations, American Bible Society, New York City.

Allen P. Wikgren, Ph.D., Associate Professor of New Testament Language and Literature, Federated Theological Faculty; Chairman, Department of New Testament and Early Christian Literature, University of Chicago.

THE PUBLISHERS

TABLE OF CONTENTS

LIST OF ABBREVIATIONS

In most articles the bibliographical references are not abbreviated, or else use abbreviations which are only partial and whose meaning is self-evident. In other articles abbreviations are used with the meanings here listed.

ABC ....*Abingdon Bible Commentary*
AJA ....*American Journal of Archaeology*
AJP ....*American Journal of Philology*
AJSL ....*American Journal of Semitic Languages*
AJT ....*American Journal of Theology*
ANF ....*Ante-Nicene Fathers*, ed. by A. C. Coxe, 8 vols., 1887; Vol. IX ed. by A. Menzies, 1897
ARG ....*Archiv fuer Reformationsgeschichte*
ASB ....*Acta sanctorum*, ed. by J. Bolland and others, Antwerp, 1643 ff.
ASOR ....American Schools of Oriental Research
ATR ....*Anglican Theological Review*
BA ....*Biblical Archaeologist*
BASOR ....*Bulletin of the American Schools of Oriental Research*
BJRL ....*Bulletin of the John Rylands Library*, Manchester
BR ....*Biblical Review*
BZAW ....*Beiheft, Zeitschrift fuer die alttestamentliche Wissenschaft*
CAH ....*Cambridge Ancient History*
CB ....*Cambridge Bible*
CHQ ....*Church Quarterly Review*
CHR ....*Catholic Historical Review*
CQ ....*Crozer Quarterly*
CSEL ....*Corpus scriptorum ecclesiasticorum Latinorum*, Vienna, 1867 ff.
CW ....*Classical Weekly*
DACL ....*Dictionnaire d'archéologie chrétienne et de liturgie*
DNB ....*Dictionary of National Biography*, ed. by L. Stephen and S. Lee, 63 vols. and supplementary vols., 1885 ff.
EB ....*Estudios Bíblicos*
EQ ....*Evangelical Quarterly*
ERE ....Hastings' *Encyclopaedia of Religion and Ethics*
ET ....*Expository Times*
Exp ....*Expositor*
HAT ....*Handbuch zum alten Testament*
HE ....*Historia ecclesiastica*
HERE ....Hastings' *Encyclopaedia of Religion and Ethics*
HKAT ....*Handkommentar zum alten Testament*, ed. by Nowack
HSAT ....*Die heilige Schrift des alten Testaments*, 4th ed., ed. by A. Bertholet
HTR ....*Harvard Theological Review*
HUCA ....*Hebrew Union College Annual*
HV ....*Historische Vierteljahrschrift*
HZAT ....*Handbuch zum alten Testament*
ICC ....*International Critical Commentary*
IJA ....*International Journal of the Apocrypha*
JAOS ....*Journal of the American Oriental Society*
JBL ....*Journal of Biblical Literature*
JBR ....*Journal of Bible and Religion*
JNES ....*Journal of Near Eastern Studies*
JourAs ....*Journal asiatique*
JQR ....*Jewish Quarterly Review*
JR ....*Journal of Religion*
JRAS ....*Journal of the Royal Asiatic Society*
JRS ....*Journal of Roman Studies*
JTS ....*Journal of Theological Studies*
KAT ....*Kommentar zum alten Testament*, ed. by Sellin
KlT ....*Kleine Texte*, ed. by H. Lietzmann
LXX ....The Septuagint
MBVP ....*Maxima bibliotheca veterum patrum, et antiquorum scriptorum ecclesiasticorum*, ed. by Marguerin de la Bigne, 27 vols., Lugduni, 1677
MGEp ....*Monumenta Germaniae historica, Epistolae*
MGH ....*Monumenta Germaniae historica*, ed. by G. H. Pertz and others, Hanover and Berlin, 1826 ff.
MPG ....J. P. Migne, *Patrologiae cursus completus, series Graeca*, 162 vols., Paris, 1857–66
MPL ....J. P. Migne, *Patrologiae cursus completus, series Latina*, 221 vols., Paris, 1844–64
NKZ ....*Neue kirchliche Zeitschrift*
NTT ....*Norsk Teologisk Tidsskrift*
OC ....*Oriens Christianus*
PG ....J. P. Migne, *Patrologiae cursus completus, series Graeca*, 162 vols., Paris, 1857–66
PL ....J. P. Migne, *Patrologiae cursus completus, series Latina*, 221 vols., Paris, 1844–64
PRE ....*Protestantische Realencyclopaedie*, Hauck-Herzog, 3rd ed.
PS ....*Patrologia syriaca*
RB ....*Revue biblique*
RBen ....*Revue bénédictine*
RE ....Pauly-Wissowa *Realencyclopaedie der klassischen Altertumswissenschaft*
RGG ....*Die Religion in Geschichte und Gegenwart*
RHE ....*Revue d'histoire ecclésiastique*
RHPR ....*Revue d'histoire et de philosophie religieuses*
RHR ....*Revue d'histoire des religions*
ROC ....*Revue de l'Orient chrétien*
RSR ....*Recherches de science religieuse*
SBA ....*Sitzungsberichte der Berliner Akademie*
SNTS ....*Studiorum Novi Testamenti Societas*
SVRG ....*Schriften des Vereins fuer Reformationsgeschichte*
ThLZ ....*Theologische Literaturzeitung*
ThSt ....*Theological Studies*
ThZts ....*Theologische Zeitschrift*
TLZ ....*Theologische Literaturzeitung*
TQ ....*Theologische Quartalschrift*
TR,NF ....*Theologische Rundschau*, Neue Folge
TT ....*Theology Today*
TU ....*Texte und Untersuchungen zur Geschichte der altchristlichen Literatur*, ed. by O. von Gebhardt and A. Harnack, 1882 ff.
TZ ....*Theologische Zeitschrift*
VC ....*Vigiliae Christianae*
WDB ....*Westminster Dictionary of the Bible*
ZATW ....*Zeitschrift fuer die alttestamentliche Wissenschaft*
ZAW ....*Zeitschrift fuer die alttestamentliche Wissenschaft*
ZDAL ....*Zeitschrift fuer deutsches Altertum und deutsche Literatur*
ZDMG ....*Zeitschrift der deutschen morgenlaendischen Gesellschaft*
ZKG ....*Zeitschrift fuer Kirchengeschichte*
ZMRW ....*Zeitschrift fuer Missionskunde und Religionswissenschaft*
ZNTW ....*Zeitschrift fuer die neutestamentliche Wissenschaft*
ZNW ....*Zeitschrift fuer die neutestamentliche Wissenschaft*
ZST ....*Zeitschrift fuer systematische Theologie*

THE TEXT OF THE BIBLE

I

BIBLE TEXT: I. The Old Testament: In recent decades archaeology and research have brought marked advances in the textual criticism of the Old Testament in uncovering new sources of knowledge and in providing a better text.

A. NEW MATERIALS: The list of modern discoveries which throw light on the Hebrew Bible includes: Aramaic incantation texts from Nippur, which reflect pre-Masoretic Hebrew characters used in Babylonia; a Hebrew text of Jeremiah 48:11, found on a jar stamp; the Lachish Letters (*q.v.*), which exhibit Hebrew script from the time of Jeremiah (589 B.C.); and the Dead Sea Scrolls (*q.v.*), embracing among other Hebrew writings the Book of Isaiah, a commentary on Habakkuk, and fragments of Leviticus. In addition, the Ras Shamra (*q.v.*) Inscriptions and the Mari Letters (*q.v.*) contribute richly to our knowledge of epigraphy, paleography, and comparative Semitic philology.

Among fragments which afford new insights into the text of the Greek Bible are: the manuscripts in the Freer Collection on Deuteronomy, Joshua, the Psalms, and Minor Prophets; the Chester Beatty Biblical Papyri (*q.v.*), which embrace parts of several books of the Old Testament in Greek antedating the leading uncials; the John Rylands Library Papyri, which afford us in portions of Deuteronomy (23–28) our earliest extant witness to the Septuagint, dated to the second century B.C.; and the John H. Scheide Papyri, representing a Greek text of Ezekiel earlier than any hitherto known.

B. TEXTUAL RESEARCH: Recent Old Testament textual criticism has included: re-evaluation of older discoveries in the light of the new; studies in comparative Semitic philology, prose, prophecy, and poetry; the alphabet, its origin, forms, consonantal mutations, and vowel values; the vocabulary, including the claims as to the composite character of Hebrew and Aramaic; pre-Masoretic and Masoretic vocalization; re-examination of the theory (Lagarde) of the archetype in the Masoretic text; efforts toward the recovery of the *Urtext,* the original Greek text of the Septuagint, and the determination of the character of the Septuagint-*Vorlage,* the text used by the translators; and intensive study of the versions.

C. CRITICAL TEXTS: Until recently all editions of the Hebrew Bible, including the first and second editions of Kittel's work (1905, 1912), were based on the printed text of Jacob ben Chayyim (1524–25). Through the work of Paul Kahle a manuscript (Leningrad Codex B 19*a*) of the Ben Asher text (tenth century) was made the basis of the third edition of Kittel's *Biblia Hebraica* (ed. by P. Kahle, A. Alt, and O. Eissfeldt, 1929–37). This is a better text than that appearing in the edition of C. D. Ginsburg (*The Old Testament Diligently Revised According to the Massorah and the Early Versions . . .*, 1926). Among other researches, Kahle's studies of manuscripts discovered in the Cairo Geniza have contributed much toward a better knowledge of the Hebrew text.

Progress toward the completion of the critical Cambridge edition of the Septuagint (*The Old Testament in Greek,* ed. by A. E. Brooke, N. McLean, and H. St. John Thackeray, 1906–) has been slow. This edition, following that of H. B. Swete, carries the text of the Codex Vaticanus, but with more extensive apparatus. In his complete edition of the Greek Bible (*Septuaginta,* 1935) A. Rahlfs provided a reconstructed text based largely on Codices Sinaiticus, Vaticanus, and Alexandrinus. The more ambitious Goettingen edition, designed by Rahlfs, is still incomplete.

BIBLIOGRAPHY: H. Bauer and P. Leander, *Historische Grammatik der hebraeischen Sprache,* 1922; A. E. Cowley, *Aramaic Papyri of the Fifth Century B.C.,* 1923; F. X. Wutz, *Die Transkriptionen von der Septuaginta bis zu Hieronymus,* 1925; *idem, Systematische Wege von der Septuaginta zum hebraeischen Urtext,* I, 1937; H. St. John Thackeray, *Some Aspects of the Greek Old Testament,* 1927; F. G. Kenyon, *The Chester Beatty Biblical Papyri,* 1933–38; *idem, The Text of the Greek Bible,* 1937; *idem, Our Bible and the Ancient Manuscripts,* 1948; L. H. Gray, *Introduction to Semitic Comparative Linguistics,* 1934; O. Eissfeldt, *Einleitung in das Alte Testament* (1934), 693 ff.; H. L. Ginsberg, *The Ugaritic Texts,* 1936; H. I. Bell, *Recent Discoveries of Biblical Papyri,* 1937; H. Torczyner, *The Lachish Letters,* 1938; A. C. Johnson, H. S. Gehman, and E. H. Kase, eds., *The John H. Scheide Biblical Papyri: Ezekiel,* 1938; C. H.

Gordon, *Ugaritic Grammar,* 1940; E. Brenno, *Studien ueber hebraeische Morphologie und Vokalismus,* 1943; D. R. Ap-Thomas, *A Primer of Old Testament Text Criticism,* 1947; Paul Kahle, *The Cairo Geniza,* 1947; G. R. Driver, *Semitic Writing,* 1948; D. Diringer, *The Alphabet,* 1948, 2nd ed., 1949; H. M. Orlinsky, *The Septuagint,* 1949; D. W. Thomas, "The Textual Criticism of the Old Testament," in *The Old Testament and Modern Study* (1951), 238–263; B. J. Roberts, *The Old Testament Text and Versions,* 1951.

[Sup.] ELMER E. FLACK.

II. The New Testament:

A. THE MANUSCRIPTS: The number of Greek witnesses to all or part of the New Testament, according to the latest official lists (published by Ernst von Dobschuetz in *Eberhard Nestle's Einfuehrung in das griechische Neue Testament,* 4te Aufl. 1923; and in *ZNTW,* XXIII [1924], 248–264; XXV [1926], 299–306; XXVI [1927], 96; XXVII [1928], 216–222; and XXXII [1933], 185–206; and by K. Aland in *TLZ* [1953], 465–496) are: papyri, 63; ostraca, 25; talismans, 9; uncial manuscripts, 232; minuscule manuscripts, 2440; and lectionaries, 1678.

The oldest known fragment of the New Testament is a tiny scrap of papyrus (designated P^{52}) measuring 2½ by 3½ inches and now at the John Rylands Library at Manchester. It contains John 18:31–33, 37–38, and has been dated by competent palaeographers within A.D. 100–150 (so C. H. Roberts, who published the fragment in 1935, and F. G. Kenyon, W. Schubart, H. I. Bell, A. Deissmann, and W. H. P. Hatch).

From the third century come the three important papyri acquired by A. Chester Beatty of Dublin and edited by Sir F. G. Kenyon (1933–37). P^{45} comprises portions of thirty leaves of a papyrus codex, which originally contained all four Gospels and Acts. Matthew and John are the least well preserved, each being represented by only two fragmentary leaves. Six leaves of Mark, seven of Luke, and thirteen of Acts remain of these books. P^{46} contains eighty-six leaves (all slightly mutilated) of a papyrus codex which originally embraced ten epistles of Paul in the following order: Rom., Heb., I and II Cor., Eph., Gal., Phil., Col., I and II Thess. P^{47} comprises ten slightly mutilated leaves of the Book of Revelation. Of the original codex, estimated to have been thirty-two leaves in length, only the middle portion remains, containing the text of 9:10–17:2. (For other papyri see B. M. Metzger, "Recently Published Greek Papyri of the New Testament," *Smithsonian Report for 1948,* pp. 439–452; and the exhaustive list of the New Testament papyri by G. Maldfeld and B. M. Metzger in *JBL,* LXVIII [1949], 359–370. See also PAPYRI, BIBLICAL AND EARLY CHRISTIAN.)

Among the more important uncial manuscripts discovered during the twentieth century are the following. Codex W, now in the Freer Collection of the Smithsonian Institution in Washington, apparently dates from the late fourth or the fifth century. It contains the Gospels in the so-called "Western" order, namely Matthew, John, Luke, Mark. The type of text changes markedly in strata, and its editor Henry A. Sanders (1912) suggested that the manuscript is descended from an ancestor made up of fragments from different rolls of the Gospels pieced together after Diocletian's attempt to destroy all Bibles.

Codex *Theta* (Koridethianus), dated by its editors, G. Beermann and C. R. Gregory (1913), in the ninth century, contains the four Gospels written in an inelegant hand by a scribe who was clearly not familiar with Greek script. Formerly it belonged to the monastery of Koridethi near the Caspian Sea, and is now in Tiflis. Its type of text (particularly in Mark) is related to that used by Origen in the third century at Caesarea. For recent discoveries of uncial fragments, see B. M. Metzger in *Expository Times,* LXIII (1951–52), 309–311, and W. H. P. Hatch in *HTR,* XLV (1952), 81–86.

B. CRITICAL EDITIONS OF THE GREEK NEW TESTAMENT: The editors of the Oxford series of Greek and Latin classics invited Alexander Souter to prepare a critical edition of the Greek New Testament with a selected critical apparatus of variant readings. His *Nouum Testamentum graece* (Oxford, 1910; ed. sec., 1947) gives the Greek text which, by inference, lies behind the English Revised Version (1881). The chief strength of the apparatus lies in the relatively full evidence from the Latin Fathers.

The most monumental edition to appear after Tischendorf's *editio octava critica maior* (1869–72) was Hermann von Soden's *Die Schriften des Neuen Testaments in ihrer aeltesten erreichbaren Textgestalt,* I. Teil: *Untersuchungen,* 1–3 Abteilungen, 1902–10; II. Teil: *Text mit Apparat,* 1913. In the first part von Soden surveys the entire history of the transmission of Greek manuscripts (excluding Greek lectionaries). According to his textual theory, most New Testament witnesses fall into one of three families, the Hesychian, Jerusalem, and Koine. He also invented a new system of sigla which indicate the age, contents, and type of text of each manuscript. Because of its complicated nature most textual critics have refused to adopt this nomenclature. His textual theory has also been criticized as involving several basic errors, such as grouping together in the Jerusalem family quite heterogeneous witnesses, and, still more serious, elevating the Koine group to a rank co-ordinate in importance with the other two groups (see K. Lake's critique in *Review of Theology and Philosophy,* IV [1908], 201–217 and 277–295). Von Soden also published a Handausgabe, *Griechisches Neues Testament, Text mit kurzen Apparat,* 1913. Two useful lists which transpose von Soden's nomenclature into the Gregory-Dobschuetz system are Friedrich Krueger's *Schluessel zu von Sodens Die Schriften des Neuen Testaments . . . ,* 1927, and Benedikt Kraft's *Die Zeichen fuer die wichtigeren Handschriften des Neuen Testaments,* 2te Aufl., 1934.

The edition prepared by Heinrich J. Vogels, *Novum Testamentum graece* (1920), makes special use of evidence derived from Old Latin, Old Syriac, and Tatianic sources. A second edition appeared in 1922; in the same year a Greek-Latin edition was published (3rd ed., 2 vols., 1949–50). For its size, August Merk's useful edition, *Novum Testamentum graece et latine* (1933; 7th ed., 1951), contains a relatively large amount of evidence of variant readings. Special attention is given to witnesses to Tatian's Diatessaron (see HARMONY OF THE GOSPELS [TATIAN'S]), but without the one-sided judgment characteristic of von Soden.

In 1935 the Oxford Press issued the first fascicle of a critical apparatus which was intended to be as comprehensive for its generation as Tischendorf's eighth edition was for his. The editor, S. C. E. Legg, published only two fascicles, *Nouum Testamentum graece secundum textum Westcotto-Hortianum; Euangelium secundum Marcum,* 1935; . . . *Euangelium secundum Matthaeum,* 1940. In 1948 the enterprise was reorganized as the International Project to Establish a Critical Edition of the Greek New Testament, with headquarters at the Universities of Chicago and Oxford.

The text of José M. Bover's *Novi Testamenti biblia graeca et latina* (1943; 3rd ed., 1953) is an eclectic one, departing frequently from an Alexandrian type of text and approaching a Western or Caesarean type. Thus it is closer to von Soden's text than to Westcott and Hort's. The apparatus, which includes the opinions of six modern editors, supplies evidence of the manuscripts on only the more important variants. (See B. M. Metzger, "Recent Spanish Contributions to the Textual Criticism of the New Testament," in *JBL,* LXVI [1947], 401–424.)

Nestle's convenient pocket edition of the Greek Testament, first published in 1898, has gone through twenty-one editions (1952). Its text is based on the readings supported by two of the following three critical editions, Tischendorf, Westcott and Hort, B. Weiss. The apparatus contains a useful and relatively full conspectus of variant readings. Graeco-Latin and Graeco-German editions have also been published.

C. DEVELOPMENTS IN TEXTUAL CRITICISM: During the twentieth century attempts were made to discover groups of manuscripts belonging to texts, families, and subgroups. K. Lake isolated family 1 (comprising manuscripts 1, 118, 131, and several others; see *Texts and Studies,* VII, 1, 1902), and several scholars have added to family 13 (comprising manuscripts 13, 69, 124, 346, 543, and others). Von Soden, despite certain methodological errors in his edition, made several noteworthy contributions, particularly in tracing the history of the text in Byzantine manuscripts. In 1924 B. H. Streeter proposed his theory of "Local Texts" (*The Four Gospels,* pp. 27–78), namely that at the great sees of antiquity there developed special, characteristic texts. They may be identified in Greek manuscripts by discovering agreements with the earliest versions and with the quotations in the earliest fathers. Streeter's findings, in abbreviated form, are as follows. The primary and secondary authorities for the five local texts: (1) Alexandria: primary = B; secondary = *aleph,* L, Sahidic, Bohairic; (2) Antioch: prim. = Sinaitic Syriac; sec. = Curetonian Syriac; (3) Caesarea: prim. = *theta,* 565 in Mark; sec. = fam. 1, fam. 13, 28, 700, W in part of Mark, Old Georgian; (4) Italy and Gaul: prim. = D; sec. = *b* and *a*; (5) Carthage: prim. = *k* in Matthew and Mark; sec. = W in part of Mark, *e*.

Streeter's work in identifying the Caesarean text was generally (though not totally) confirmed and supplemented by a monograph entitled, "The Caesarean Text of the Gospel of Mark," by K. Lake, R. P. Blake, and Silva New (*HTR,* XXI [1928], 207–404). Not the least important part of these scholars' work was the attention they give to certain oriental versions, namely the Old Armenian, the Old Georgian, and the Palestinian Syriac, all of which, in their opinion, are witnesses to the Caesarean text.

Subsequent investigation, particularly after the discovery of the Chester Beatty Biblical Papyri, has tended to modify these opinions in the direction of dividing the Caesarean text into the primitive or pre-Caesarean group (including P^{45}, W, fam. 1, 28, and fam. 13), and the recensional or Caesarean group proper (including *theta,* 565, 700, Origen, Eusebius, the Sinaitic Syriac, Old Armenian, and Old Georgian); see especially Teófilo Ayuso in *Biblica,* XVI (1935), 369–415. For a survey of the problems up to 1945, see B. M. Metzger, "The Caesarean Text of the Gospels," *JBL,* LXIV (1945), 457–489; subsequent treatments include A. H. White, "The Problem of the Caesarean Text," *Journal of the Manchester University Egypt and Orient Society,* XXIV, 1942–45 (published in 1947), 39–59; Francesco Russo, "I manoscritti del gruppo 'Ferrar,'" *Bollettina della badia greca di Grottaferrata,* N.S. III (1949), 76–90; and Lars-Olov Almgren, "Diskussionen om den caesarensiska texttypen," *Svensk exegetisk årsbok,* XV (1950), 81–100.

Another area which hitherto has been almost totally neglected by textual critics, the Greek Gospel lectionaries, has recently begun to receive more attention (see LECTIONARIES, NEW TESTAMENT GREEK, and H. Greeven, *ThLZ,* LXXVI [1951], cols. 513–522).

The so-called Western text remains the *bête noire* of New Testament textual critics. In reaction to the generally unfavorable regard which Westcott and Hort had for this type of text, certain scholars (e.g., J. R. Harris, F. C. Burkitt, Hans von Soden, A. C. Clark, H. J. Vogels,

Alexander Souter, H. A. Sanders, C. H. Turner), held in varying degrees to the general superiority of the Western text. At present textual critics of the New Testament recognize that the Western text undoubtedly contains some original readings not present in other types of text, but few would agree (with A. C. Clark and H. A. Sanders) that its readings are almost always to be preferred. On the contrary, they would either continue to regard (with K. Lake, J. H. Ropes, W. H. P. Hatch) the Neutral or Alexandrian form of text as generally superior to all others, or would be (with L. Vaganay, H. Pernot, and E. C. Colwell) frankly eclectic. See A. F. J. Klijn, *A Survey of the Researches into the Western Text of the Gospels and Acts,* 1949 (with additional bibliography by Metzger in *Theologische Zeitschrift,* VII [1951], 330). On methodology in general see Metzger, "Trends in the Textual Criticism of the Iliad, the Mahābhārata, and the New Testament," *JBL,* LXV (1946), 339–352.

Bibliography: Handbooks of New Testament textual criticism include: Caspar René Gregory, *The Canon and Text of the New Testament,* 1907; Edward A. Hutton, *An Atlas of Textual Criticism,* 1911; F. G. Kenyon, *Handbook to the Textual Criticism of the New Testament,* 2nd ed., 1912; Alexander Souter, *The Text and Canon of the New Testament,* 1912; E. Jacquier, *Le Nouveau Testament dans l'église chrétienne,* II, *Le texte du Nouveau Testament,* 10th ed., 1913; P. G. Groenen, *Algemeene inleiding tot de heilige schrift,* II, *Geschiedenis van den tekst,* 1917; August Pott, *Der Text des Neuen Testaments nach seiner geschichtlichen Entwicklung,* 2nd ed., 1919; Ernst von Dobschuetz, *Eberhard Nestles Einfuehrung in das griechische Neue Testament,* 4th ed., 1923; H. J. Vogels, *Handbuch der neutestamentlichen Textkritik,* 1923; A. T. Robertson, *An Introduction to the Textual Criticism of the New Testament,* 1925; 2nd ed., 1928; K. Lake, *The Text of the New Testament,* 6th ed., rev. by Silva New, 1928; Giuseppe Sacco, *La koinè del Nuovo Testamento e la trasmissione del sacro testo,* 1928; Leon Vagnay, *Initiation à la critique textuelle neotestamentaire,* 1934, Eng. trans., *An Introduction to the Textual Criticism of the New Testament,* 1937; M. J. Lagrange, *Introduction à l'étude du Nouveau Testament;* II, *Critique textuelle,* 2, *La critique rationnelle,* 1935; F. G. Kenyon, *The Text of the Greek Bible, A Students Handbook,* 1937. For 1200 additional works, see B. M. Metzger, *Annotated Bibliography of the Textual Criticism of the New Testament,* 1955. See also Bible Versions, I; and Harmony of the Gospels (Tatian's).

[Sup.] Bruce M. Metzger.

II

DEAD SEA SCROLLS: I. The Discovery: The manuscripts known as the Dead Sea Scrolls were discovered by an Arab goatherd early in 1947 in a cave near the northwest corner of the Dead Sea. Five were sold to Mar Athanasius Yeshue Samuel, the Syrian Orthodox Metropolitan, at St. Mark's Monastery in Jerusalem, six to Professor E. L. Sukenik of the Hebrew University. Each purchased also several fragments of manuscripts.

The cave was visited by individuals, but not until the early months of 1949 was it scientifically excavated by G. L. Harding of the Department of Antiquities of Jordan and Father R. de Vaux of the Dominican École Biblique at Jerusalem. No more manuscripts were found, but hundreds of fragments were uncovered. Other fragments have since been acquired by the Palestine Museum at Jerusalem.

Two of the scrolls bought by the Syrian Metropolitan are parts of the Manual of Discipline of a Jewish sect. One is a complete copy of the book of Isaiah; another contains a commentary on Habakkuk. The fifth is in bad condition and has not been unrolled. One column has been detached; it is in Aramaic and consists of apocalyptic material, possibly from the lost Apocalypse of Lamech. The fragments purchased by Archbishop Samuel include two from the book of Daniel. Of the scrolls bought by Professor Sukenik, one contains part of the book of Isaiah, one a composition called the War of the Sons of Light with the Sons of Darkness, and the other three psalms of thanksgiving. The fragments excavated include bits of Genesis, Deuteronomy, and Judges, four in an archaic script from Leviticus, and a scrap of the book of Jubilees in Hebrew. Among the fragments purchased by the Palestine Museum are portions of the Manual of Discipline.

II. Date: The date of the manuscripts is disputed, but evidence of several kinds is available. The excavation showed that the manuscripts had been placed in large jars of the Hellenistic period. A few pieces of Roman pottery suggested that the cave had been entered during the Roman period. The manuscripts may have been more or less ancient than the jars; the excavators believe, however, that all were deposited in the cave before 100 B.C. Other archaeologists lower the limit to about 25 B.C.

The materials used afford a general indication of date. The radiocarbon method of dating ancient materials cannot be applied to the scrolls themselves because it involves the destruction of the material; some of the linen in which the scrolls were wrapped has been examined by this process, however, and dated between 167 B.C. and A.D. 233.

Two literary references to similar discoveries in the same region have been noted by scholars. Eusebius says that a manuscript used by Origen was found in a jar at Jericho; nothing is said of a cave, and the text in question was not Hebrew but Greek. A discovery of Hebrew manuscripts in a cave near Jericho about A.D. 800 is related in a letter of Timotheus, Metropolitan of Seleucia. This may have been the same cave that was discovered in 1947.

Paleography provides evidence of the age of the scrolls. Lack of exactly dated material for comparison prevents precise dating on this basis, but the material is sufficient to make wholly improbable a date earlier than 150 B.C. for the oldest of the scrolls (except perhaps the Leviticus fragments in archaic script) or later than A.D. 150 for the youngest of them.

The original compositions are of course older than the manuscripts containing them. Aside from the books of the Old Testament, when the writings contained in the scrolls were composed must be determined by internal evidence, including references to historical persons and events. The War of the Sons of Light with the Sons of Darkness gives directions for a conflict which may be either historical or eschatological but cannot be identified with any known war. The Kittim in this document seem to be the Macedonian rulers of Egypt and Syria. In the Habakkuk Commentary, however, the Kittim are the Romans. The Commentary, like the Damascus Document, speaks of a Teacher of Righteousness. He was persecuted by a Wicked Priest. A Man of the Lie is mentioned also, and a group called the House of Absalom is condemned for not helping the Teacher of Righteousness. Many attempts to identify all these have been made, but none as yet is convincing. A passage in the Habakkuk Commentary is interpreted by Dupont-Sommer as referring to the capture of Jerusalem by Pompey in 63 B.C., but his interpretation is unacceptable. The historical references have not yet yielded any clear clue to the date of the compositions.

The language of the documents tells something of their place in the history of the Hebrew language. In general it is similar to that of the latest books of the Old Testament, but goes farther than any of them or any other extant Hebrew literature.

In religious terminology and sometimes in extended passages the documents are closely related to the Damascus Document and evidently come from the same group. Affinities with the Apocrypha and Pseudepigrapha, with the rabbinic literature, and even with that of the medieval Karaites have been noted. In the religious ideas and practices and the moral ideals of the group may be found evidence concerning its place in the history of Judaism. The interpretation of Scripture, the calendar, the organization and rites of the group, its apocryphal and messianic ideas, its dualism and angelology, and its attitudes toward war, marriage, and wealth are all significant. Even these, however, do not enable us to establish the chronological position of these writings in Jewish history.

The group represented by the Dead Sea Scrolls and the Damascus Document has been identified by scholars with the pre-Maccabean Hasidim, with some branch of the Pharisees in the Hasmonean period, with the Essenes, with an obscure group called Magharians (cave people), with the followers of Zadok the Pharisee at the time of the destruction of the temple, and with the Christian Ebionites, not to mention the Karaites. Much research will be necessary before the evidence and arguments for all these theories can be sifted and the possibilities and probabilities duly weighed.

III. Significance: Meanwhile it is clear that the scrolls are important in many ways. The Isaiah manuscripts and to a lesser extent some of the other documents are important sources for the textual criticism of the Old Testament. In the Syrian Isaiah manuscript especially we have now a pre-Masoretic Hebrew text, poorly copied and full of errors but containing also real variants, some of which may be superior to the Masoretic readings. These manuscripts afford entirely new knowledge of the vulgar forms of the Old Testament text which circulated alongside the more carefully guarded quasi-official tradition.

For the history of Judaism the significance of the scrolls is great, even though we cannot precisely date them or exactly identify the group which produced them. They testify to the variety and richness of Jewish beliefs, traditions, and practices in the period between the completion of the Old Testament and the definite establishment of "normative" orthodox Judaism. The covenanters of Judea were one of many lateral branches of the family tree of Judaism which did not survive but which bore fruit for later periods of the religion.

The bearing of the documents on Christian origins and early history is important also, though it has been exaggerated by a few scholars. Antecedents and parallels for terms and ideas which appear in the New Testament and other Christian writings appear in the scrolls. In general, however, it is just the importance of the scrolls for Judaism in the Hellenistic or Roman period which makes them most important for Christian history.

Bibliography: The periodic literature on the scrolls is already enormous. Only book titles are given here. Millar Burrows, John Trever, and William Brownlee, *The Dead Sea Scrolls of St. Mark's Monastery*, I, 1950; II, fasc. 2, 1951; A Dupont-Sommer, *Aperçus préliminaires sur les Monuscrits de la Mer Morte*, 1950; *Observations sur le Commentaire d'Habacus découvert près de la Mer Morte*, 1950; *Observations sur le Manuel de Discipline découvert près de la Mer Morte*, 1951; Paul Kahle, *Die Hebraeischen Handschriften aus der Hoehle*, 1951; E. L. Sukenik, *Megillot Genuzot*, I, 1948; II, 1950; Mier Wallenstein, *Hymns from the Judean Scrolls*, 1950.

Millar Burrows.

III

PAPYRI, BIBLICAL AND EARLY CHRISTIAN: The extensive discovery and publication of papyri within the last half century has had a continuing and growing significance for the study and interpretation of early Christianity and its literature. New evidence for the biblical text has emerged in unexpected quantity, and the philological and historical backgrounds of the Bible have been illuminated by the many documents reflecting the everyday life and language of that era. An estimated 25,000 or more papyri are now known, about half of which have been published.

In the Old Testament some fragments of pre-Masoretic text have appeared on Babylonian incantation bowls and elsewhere, but the Nash papyrus remains the only considerable fragment of Hebrew on papyrus. Recent study has tended to date it in an earlier period than hitherto generally proposed, even as early as the second century B.C.

In the matter of Greek papyri we are much more fortunate. When A. Rahlfs published his *Verzeichnis der griechischen Handschriften des Alten Testaments* in 1914 he was able to list some fifty different papyri ranging in date from the second or third to the seventh century A.D. But most of the documents were very fragmentary, only half a dozen containing any extensive amount of text. Among these were the fourth-century roll containing Psalms 30–55 in mutilated condition (MS 2013) edited by C. F. Heinrici in 1903 and a valuable codex of Genesis from the third or fourth century A.D. (MS 911). Since 1914 about fifteen new documents have come to light, some with texts surpassing any known papyri in significance. A codex of the Minor Prophets (MS "X"), purchased in 1916 by Charles Freer, was published by H. A. Sanders and Carl Schmidt in 1927 together with the above-mentioned Genesis, which had appeared at Akhmim in 1906. The famous Beatty papyri, a group of eight manuscripts of the Old Testament, three of the New, and one of portions of I Enoch and a Christian homily were purchased by A. Chester Beatty in Egypt in 1931. These documents provided a second Septuagint text of Daniel and the last ten chapters of the Book of Enoch, hitherto unknown in Greek. A large part of the Ezekiel text, earlier in form than any previously known, was separately acquired by the American collector, John H. Scheide, who deposited it in Princeton University. Of unusual interest because of their early date (*ca.* 150 B.C.) are the fragments of two Deuteronomic rolls, one of which is in Manchester and the other in Cairo. The former was published by C. H. Roberts in 1936.

The following is a list of the more significant documents. The numbers are those assigned by Rahlfs or by W. Kappler, who continued his listing. All are codices unless otherwise indicated.

- X. Minor prophets (Amos 1:10—Mal.), iii cen., Washington, D. C.
- 905. Gen. 14–15, 19–20, 24–27, iii cen., Oxford.
- 911. Gen. 1:16—35:8, iii-iv cen., Berlin.
- 919. Minor prophets (Zech. 4:6—Mal. 4:5), vii cen., Heidelberg.
- 957. Deut. 23–26, 28, ii cen. B.C., Manchester.
- 961. Gen. 9:1—44:22, iv cen., London, Beatty Collection.
- 962. Gen. 8:13—9:1; 24:13—25:21; 30:24—46:33, iii cen., Beatty Collection.
- 963. Deut. and Num. (fragments), ii cen., Beatty Collection.
- 964. Eccl. 36:28—37:22; 46:6–11, 16—47:2, iv cen., Beatty Collection.
- 965. Isa. (fragments, especially of chaps. 8–19, 38–45, 54–60), iii cen., Beatty Collection.
- 966. Jer. 4:30—5:1, 9–24, ii cen., Beatty Collection.
- 967, 968. Ezek. 11:25—17:21; Dan. 3:72—8:27; Esth. 2:20—8:6, iii cen., Beatty Collection. Ezek. 19:12—39:29, iii cen., Princeton.
- 2013. Pss. 30–55, iv cen., roll, Leipzig.
- 2019. Pss. 11 (12):7—14 (15):4, iii cen., roll, London.
- 2055. Pss. 143 (144):14—148:3, iii-iv cen., location uncertain.
- (?). Deut. 31:28—32:7, ii cen. B.C., roll, Cairo.

The following are some important papyri of the versions: Deuteronomy, Jonah, Acts, Sahidic, iv cen., London.

Song of Songs, Lamentations, Proverbs, Sahidic, iii-iv cen., Hamburg.

Psalms, Sahidic, vi-vii cen., London.

Psalms, Georgian, vii-viii cen., Mt. Sinai.

The most significant New Testament documents are the Beatty papyri ($P^{45, 46, 47}$). An excellent facsimile and text edition of these was published in 1933–41 by Sir Frederic Kenyon. There are about sixty other known papyri ranging in date from the third to the seventh century. While mostly fragments, they throw considerable light on the textual situation in that period. Of the Gospels there are twenty-five manuscripts; of Acts, twelve; Paul, sixteen; Hebrews, four; the Catholic Epistles, four; Revelation, four. In 1935 some second-century fragments of an "unknown gospel" related to our Gospels were published by Bell and Skeat. In the following list of the more extensive and earlier documents we follow the Gregory-von Dobschuetz enumeration. (Many of the papyri are fragmentary within the chapters specified.) Recent listings by Maldfeld and Metzger give further details of description and other data.

P4 Luke 1:58—6:16, iv cen., lectionary, Paris.
P6 John 10:1—11:52, v-vi cen., Strassburg.
P8 Acts 4:31—6:15, iv cen., Berlin.
P15 I Cor. 7:18—8:4, iv cen., Cairo.
P16 Phil. 3:9—4:8, iv cen., Cairo.
P19 Matt. 10:32—11:5, v cen., Oxford.
P20 James 2:19—3:9, iii cen., Princeton.
P22 John 15:25—16:31, iii cen., roll, Glasgow.
P37 Matt. 26:19–52, iii cen., Ann Arbor, Mich.
P38 Acts 18:27—19:16, iii-iv cen., Ann Arbor.
P44 Matt. 17:1—18:19; 25:8–10; John 9:3—10:11; 12:17–18, vi-vii cen., lectionary, New York.
P45 Matt. 20–21; 25–26; Mark 4–9; 11–12; Luke 6–7; 9–14; John 10–11; Acts 4–17, iii cen., Vienna and London.
P46 Rom. 5–6; 8–16; Heb.; I and II Cor.; Eph.; Gal.; Phil.; Col.; I Thess. 1–2; 5, iii cen., Ann Arbor and London.
P47 Rev. 9:10—17:2, iii cen., London.
P48 Acts 23:11–29, iii cen., Florence.
P52 John 18:31—34, 37–38, ii cen., Manchester.
P59 John 1–2; 11–12; 17–18; 21, vii cen., New York.
P60 John 16:29—19:26, same.
P61 Rom. 16; I Cor. 1, 5; Phil. 3; Col. 1, 4; I Thess. 1; Titus 3; Philem., same.

Among the previously listed papyri (Vol. VIII, p. 343) it should be noted that No. 24 (P11) is now in the State Public Library, Leningrad, and No. 26 (P12) is in the Pierpont Morgan Library, New York.

Of the versions, several papyri have been discovered. Most important are the fourth century Sahidic Acts already mentioned, a Sahidic manuscript of Acts and the Pauline Epistles (*ca.* A.D. 600), and a "sub-Akhmimic" text of John from the fourth century. The last two were published by Sir Herbert Thompson in 1932 and 1924 respectively.

In the area of early Christian literature some amazing discoveries have been made within the last few decades. Especially noteworthy are the third-century, Ann Arbor codex containing a fourth of the Greek text of the Shepherd of Hermas; eleven pages of the hitherto missing conclusion of the Acts found in a Hamburg papyrus (Oxy. 1919) of about A.D. 300; an almost complete text of the lost homily of Melito of Sardis "On the Passion" discovered in 1940 among the Beatty papyri in the University of Michigan; a Cairo manuscript containing a Coptic text of the Epistle of the Apostles; and twelve Coptic codices of over a thousand pages containing forty-two Gnostic treatises—thirty-seven complete—discovered in upper Egypt in 1946.

An extensive amount of very fragmentary material has also come to light. This includes, besides the first three of the above-named, portions of I Clement, Ignatius, Aristides, Irenaeus, Hippolytus, Acts of John, Protevangelium, Gospel of Mary, Apocalypse of Elias, the Abgar-Jesus letters, and a few hagiographa. To the "agrapha" may be added an Oxyrhynchus papyrus (no. 1384) of the fifth century containing a saying of Jesus on curing the sick. About twenty-five "libelli" or certificates of loyalty are now known, for the most part supposedly Christian and dating from the Decian persecution. Other documents and scraps represent letters, homilies, prayers, hymns, creeds, liturgical pieces, amulets, and the like, a large number of which are Coptic. Many contain biblical quotations and allusions, and all are of great interest in their reflection of early Christian life and faith.

See also CANON OF SCRIPTURE, II, C; HYMNS IN THE EARLY CHURCH, II; JESUS CHRIST, PICTURES AND IMAGES OF; STENOGRAPHY AND CHURCH HISTORY.

BIBLIOGRAPHY: Harold Idris Bell, *Recent Discoveries of Biblical Papyri*, 1937; Camden M. Cobern, *The New Archeological Discoveries and Their Bearing Upon the New Testament*, 5th ed., 1921; Frederic G. Kenyon, *Our Bible and the Ancient Manuscripts*, 4th ed., 1939; Georg Maldfeld and Bruce M. Metzger, "Detailed List of Greek Papyri of the New Testament," in *JBL*, LXVIII (1949), 359-370; John Garrett Winter, *Life and Letters in the Papyri*, 1933; George Milligan, *Here and There Among the Papyri*, 1922; J. Jeremias, "Der gegenwaertige Stand der fruehchristlichen Papyrologie," in *Theol. Literaturzeitung*, LXXV (1950), 55 ff.

[Sup.] ALLEN P. WIKGREN.

IV

LECTIONARIES, NEW TESTAMENT GREEK: The lectionaries of the Greek New Testament contain most of the text except Revelation and part of Acts arranged in selections designed to supply readings for the liturgical year of the church. (For the general contents and organization of these documents see EVANGELIARIUM, Vol. IV, and PERICOPE, Vol. VIII.) Known Greek lectionaries now total about 1700. They include a large number of uncial documents ranging in date from the seventh to the twelfth centuries and a dozen leaves and fragments from the fourth to sixth, of which five or six are papyri.

The origin of the lectionary still remains obscure. We are ignorant of the exact circumstances and date of the transition from early usage of nonlectionary manuscripts with lections marked off in the text to the later lectionary proper. The papyri do not appear to reflect the organization of lections as we know them from the seventh century on. However, various converging lines of evidence, historical, liturgical and textual, point to Syria, possibly Antioch, in the mid-fourth century as a likely place and date for this event.

This and other problem areas are receiving illumination from recent textual research. Although some scholars, especially Gregory and Scrivener, appreciated the potential value of lectionaries for the study and reconstruction of the New Testament text, they were generally neglected or inadequately employed to this end until recently. Critical and systematic exploration of their text began at Chicago in the 1930's, in particular with the publication of the lectionary studies edited by Colwell and Riddle in 1933. This volume may be consulted with profit for data on terminology, contents, method of study, textual evaluation, and previous use of lectionaries. Here and in subsequent studies (see Bibliography) the key to the text was shown to be the individual lection as the unit for analysis. Quality of text was found to vary by lections or groups of lections, while, at the same time, a remarkable homogeneity of text was displayed in such lections, irrespective of the date of the manuscripts. While this text is predominantly "Byzantine" in large areas, certain groups of lessons are found to have an early form characterized usually by "Alexandrian" and "Caesarean" readings. This points to the fourth century as the time of fixation of the text, the conservative nature of these "pulpit Bibles" accounting for the preservation of the early readings in spite of a tendency for assimilation to the later ecclesiastical forms. Lectionaries also had their influence upon non-lectionary manuscripts, significant examples being the location of John 7:53–8:11 after Luke 21 and Luke 22:43–44 after Matt. 26:39 in the group of minuscules known as Family 13.

Further textual research has been stimulated of late by the international project to establish a new *apparatus criticus* to the Greek New Testament. Here for the first time lectionaries will be accorded adequate recognition and consistent representation. The ultimate aim of lectionary study remains the establishment of a critical text. The Patriarchate edition is uncritical, being marked by frequent assimilation to the current ecclesiastical form.

BIBLIOGRAPHY: Ernest C. Colwell, "Is There a Lectionary Text of the Gospels?" in *HTR*, XXV (1932), 73–84; Ernest C. Colwell and Donald W. Riddle (eds.), *Studies in the Lectionary Text:* Vol. I, *Prolegomena*, 1933; Vol. II, No. 1, Rodney Branton, *The Common Text of the Gospel Lectionary in the Lenten Lections*, 1934; No. 2, Morgan W. Redus, *The Text of the Major Festivals of the Menologion in the Greek Gospel Lectionary*, 1936; No. 3, Bruce M. Metzger, *The Saturday and Sunday Lessons from Luke in the Greek Gospel Lectionary*, 1944; Vol. III, Allen P. Wikgren (ed.), No. 1, William Bray, *The Week Day Lessons from Luke in the Greek Lectionary.*

ALLEN P. WIKGREN.

THE CANON OF THE BIBLE

V

CANON OF SCRIPTURE: I. Old Testament: In the course of its history the term "canon" (Greek, *kanōn,* "rod"; Hebrew, *qāneh,* "reed") has acquired a variety of meanings. Originally a straight rod, it came to signify anything straight—a rule, standard, model, measure, criterion, or norm. Then it came to mean a rule of faith. While the Hebrews regarded their Scriptures as inspired, they did not refer to them as "canonical." Church fathers in the fourth century A.D. first applied the term to the sacred Scriptures to distinguish them as the authoritative writings recognized by the church. The crystallization of what is now the Old Testament was a long and complicated process, marked by several stages. Modern research has thrown considerable light on the process.

A. THE FIRST STAGE: Cultic interests in Israel contributed much toward the recognition of sacred writings. The religious community gradually crystallized, collected, and preserved early songs, narratives, laws, annals, psalms, prophecies, and other literary remains (see Ex. 40:20; Deut. 31:24–26). Men of God gave forth utterances recognized at once as inspired. So there was no early demand for a formal canonization. The first public recognition which the Hebrews gave a sacred document seems to have taken place in 621 B.C. when "the book of the law" which Hilkiah found in the temple was formally made regulative by pronouncement of King Josiah (II Kings 23:1 ff.) This marked the beginning of the subtle process which in time brought public recognition of the tripartite canon. Scholars are not agreed as to the time each of the three parts received formal approval. Pfeiffer, e.g., suggests that the canonization of the Law took place *ca.* 400 B.C.; the Prophets, *ca.* 200 B.C.; and the Hagiographa, finally *ca.* A.D. 90. Oesterley and Robinson, following Hoelscher, find no canon of the Old Testament before the Council of Jamnia, *ca.* A.D. 90. G. R. Driver questions the theory that the issue was settled at Jamnia. Rowley and many others feel that the fixation of the canon was by general consent and not by formal decision.

Doubtless, the Torah (*q.v.*) acquired earliest recognition as authoritative. Long after the crystallization of the Prophets and the Writings the primacy of the Pentateuch prevailed. The fixation of the literary strata and eventually the books of the Pentateuch (*q.v.*) was an involved process. Apparently it was complete by the time of Nehemiah (432 B.C.), for when the Samaritans withdrew from Judaism (Neh. 13:28 f.), they adopted the Pentateuch as their sole canon. At least by *ca.* 250 B.C., when the Torah was translated into Greek (the Septuagint, *q.v.*), it had become the Bible of Judaism. In all the synagogues the Law was read and regarded as authoritative.

B. THE PROPHETIC COLLECTION: Continued in the "Former Prophets" is the historical narrative begun in the Pentateuch. Within this prophetic framework numerous documents sprang up only to be lost in the process of selection, evaluation, assimilation, and preservation (I Kings 11:41; 14:19, 29; I Chron. 29:29). Evidently the Deuteronomists organized, adapted, and edited these materials during the Exile (*ca.* 550 B.C.) to preserve the prophetic record of the history and faith of Israel, which had become vitiated by the fall of Jerusalem in 587 B.C. Later hands made numerous alterations in the text.

The "Latter Prophets" had a somewhat different development. Projected for the most part independently and limited in their early use by reason of the primacy of the Law, the writings of the prophets acquired public recognition slowly. During the Exile, under the influence of Ezekiel (*q.v.*) and the Second Isaiah (*q.v.*), who projected great hopes for Israel's future, there sprang up a revival of interest in prophecy, particularly predictive passages envisioning the coming of a Deliverer and the overthrow of Israel's enemies. As reverence for the written Law increased, there came also a growing appreciation of the word of the prophet. But in spite of this, countless interpolations were made in the text to bring books up to date and to enhance their values for current religion and morality. The presence of late sections in some prophecies and the absence of the Book of Daniel (*q.v.*) from the collection place the fixation of the prophetic canon late, *ca.* 200 B.C. Writing *ca.* 180 B.C., Ben Sira reveals a recognition of "the Law and the Prophets" (Ecclus. 44–49). In 132 B.C. the grandson of Ben Sira refers repeatedly to these two divisions, both of which by that time had been translated into Greek.

C. THE HAGIOGRAPHA: The process by which the "Writings" attained canonical status was much more imperceptible than that attending the Law and the Prophets. This was due to their independent character, varied contents, and loose connection. About all that they had in common was the claim of inspiration. Each faced its own problem of survival. Wide appeal and circulation insured their ultimate preservation. Some of the books, such as Psalms and Proverbs, include separate collections. By 132 B.C. there existed a fluid grouping, for Ben Sira's grandson refers to "the Law and the Prophets and the rest of the books." But while the third division in general had become crystallized before the beginning of the Christian era (see Luke 24:44), some of the books, such as Esther (*q.v.*), Ecclesiastes (*q.v.*), and the Song of Solomon (*q.v.*), remained long under dispute. The fate of Jerusalem in A.D. 70, the disorganization of Judaism, controversies over the status of certain books, and the influence of Christianity led to the fixation of the canon of twenty-four books (twenty-two, with Ruth combined with Judges and Lamentations with Jeremiah). The formal recognition of the complete Old Testament is usually regarded as having taken place at the Council of Jamnia, *ca.* A.D. 90, though the general pattern appeared much earlier and some books came into question later.

D. THE GREEK BIBLE: Besides the twenty-four canonical books (thirty-nine in the English Bible), there are numerous documents of the last centuries B.C. and the first century A.D. classified as the Apocrypha and Pseudepigrapha of the Old Testament (*qq.v.*). In recent decades these writings have become the object of considerable research. It has been observed that Jews in Alexandria handled Scripture more loosely than did those in Palestine. The latter held that prophecy ended in the time of Ezra (Neh. 8 f.), thus precluding admission to canonical standing of any document recognized as later; the former, on the other hand, held to the continuity of inspiration and the sanctity of books translated from Hebrew or Aramaic into Greek. Hence they included in their loose collection not only the books of the Hebrew canon but also the Apocrypha, which they interspersed among the canonical writings and made numerous other alterations in the text. But apparently they did not set up a special Alexandrian canon. The witness of the Septuagint is to the effect that the Old Testament canon had not become fixed when the Greek version was projected. Bentzen, following Kahle, suggests that the Greek Bible was the creation of the Christian Church.

E. CHRISTIAN USAGE: The New Testament bears testimony to the free use of Scripture on the part of early Christians. It includes, besides numerous quotations from each of the three parts of the Old Testament, adduced largely, though not exclusively, from the Septuagint, several references to or reminiscences of writings lying outside the Hebrew canon (see Heb. 11:35–37; James 1:19; Jude vv. 5, 14–16.) This practice of employing a larger collection obtains also in the writings of the apostolic and early church fathers. While the Septuagint was the Old Testament long used by the church, the acceptance of the Apocrypha was by no means universal. There was, in fact, considerable variation in usage in both East and West. Jerome, e.g., protested vigorously against the inclusion of these books, but Augustine and the Roman Church, following him, accepted them. At the time of the Reformation the Protestant churches returned to the original Palestinian canon as the basis for doctrine, but retained the arrangement of books as handed down by the Septuagint and the Vulgate, which leave no distinction between the second and third divisions of the tripartite canon. In his German Bible of 1534 Luther placed the Apocrypha at the end of the Old Testament, with the notation that they were inferior but "good and useful for reading."

Modern research has brought fresh appreciation of the intertestamental literature and likewise a better understanding of the complex process by which the canon of Scripture became established under divine direction.

BIBLIOGRAPHY: M. L. Margolis, *The Hebrew Scriptures in the Making,* 1922; H. E. Ryle, *The Canon of the Old Testament,* 2nd ed., 1925; S. Zeitlin, *An Historical Study of the Canonization of the Hebrew Scriptures,* 1933; Otto Eissfeldt, *Einleitung in das Alte Testament* (1934), pp. 614–630; W. O. E. Oesterley and T. H. Robinson, *An Introduction to the Books of the Old Testament* (1934), pp. 1–10; R. H. Pfeiffer, *Introduction to the Old Testament* (1941), pp. 50–70; Aage Bentzen, *Introduction to the Old Testament,* Vol. I (1948), pp. 20–41; Artur Weiser, *Einleitung in das Alte Testament* (1949), pp. 243–256; H. H. Rowley, *The Growth of the Old Testament,* 1950; Gunnar Ostborn, *Cult and Canon: A Study in the Canonization of the Old Testament,* 1951; Arthur Jeffrey, "The Canon of the Old Testament," *The Interpreter's Bible,* Vol. I (1952), pp. 32–45.

[Sup.] ELMER E. FLACK.

II. New Testament: A. DOCUMENTS AND LISTS RELATING TO THE CANON: (1) The Marcionite Prologues to the (ten) Pauline Epistles. In 1907 Donatien De Bruyne showed ("Prologue biblique d'origine marcionite," *RBén,* XXIV, 1–16) that the Prologues or prefatory statements regarding the authorship, place of origin, purpose, and occasion of writing, which are found widely spread in certain Vulgate manuscripts of the Pauline Epistles, originated in Marcion's canon of "the Apostolos," comprising originally Galatians, Corinthians, Romans, Thessalonians, Laodiceans, Colossians, Philippians, and Philemon. Characteristically the Prologues lay great stress on Paul's work in correcting the teaching of "false apostles." At once J. R. Harris (*ET,* XVIII [1907], 393–394), A. von Harnack (*TLZ* [1907], cols. 138–140), and F. C. Burkitt (*The Gospel History and Its Transmission* [2nd ed., 1907], pp. 353–357) acclaimed the brilliance of De Bruyne's investigation and adduced evidence for believing that the Prologues were written originally in Greek. Later the Catholic Church took over these Prologues practically unaltered, substituted "Ephesians" for "Laodiceans," and added Prologues to II Corinthians, II Thessalonians, I Timothy, II Timothy, and Titus. Last of all (probably not before A.D. 350–380) a Prologue was provided for Hebrews; the wording of this differs markedly among the manuscripts, at least six different forms being extant.

The attempt by W. Mundel ("Die Herkunft der 'marcionitischen' Prologe," *ZNTW,* XXIV [1925], 56–77) to prove that these Prologues are not of Marcionite origin, but are probably dependent upon Ambrosiaster (*q.v.*), has failed to carry conviction (see Harnack's refutation, *ZNTW,* XXIV [1925], 204–218; cf. also E. Barnikol, "Marcions Paulusbriefprologe," *Theologische Jahrbuecher,* VI [1938], 15–16).

The text of the original Prologues, with an English translation, is given by Burkitt, *op. cit.*, and reprinted by John Knox, *Marcion and the New Testament,* 1942.

(2) The Anti-Marcionite Gospel Prologues. These Prologues to the Gospels of Mark, Luke, and John (the Matthean Preface has been lost) are extant in 12, 33, and 10 Latin manuscripts respectively, dating from the fifth to the tenth century. In addition, the Prologue to Luke is extant also in Greek, preserved in two manuscripts from the tenth and eleventh centuries. In 1928 Donatien De Bruyne ("Les plus anciens Prologues latins des Évangiles," *RBén,* XL [1928], 193–214) perceived their anti-Marcionite tendency and argued that they were written originally in Greek between A.D. 160 and 180 in opposition to Marcion. Harnack immediately adopted De Bruyne's findings and pointed out further implications of statements in the Prologues bearing on the Lucan authorship of Acts, the Johannine and apostolic authorship of Revelation, and Luke's relation to Paul ("Die aeltesten Evangelien-Prologe und die Bildung des NTs," *SBA,* phil.-hist. Kl., XXIV [1928], 322–341). The statement in the Prologue to the Gospel of John, that Papias in his (lost) *Expositions* asserted that the Fourth Gospel was written in the lifetime of John and taken down at his dictation by Papias, has aroused much discussion. (a) W. F. Howard ("The Anti-Marcionite Prologues to the Gospels," *ET,* XLVII [1935–36], 534–538) favored Lightfoot's conjecture that an ambiguous form of the Greek verb was wrongly taken to mean that Papias was John's amanuensis. (b) Robert Eisler (*The Enigma of the Fourth Gospel,* 1938) emended the Prologue to make it assert that John dictated his Gospel to Marcion (see H. Burnaby's refutation, *JTS,* XLI [1940], 295–300). (c) F. L. Cross (in a letter to *The* [London] *Times,* February 10, 1936) thought that the Prologue, in its presumed original form, "asserted that the Fourth Gospel was written by John the Elder at the dictation of John the Apostle when the latter had reached a very old age." (d) Engelbert Gutwenger, S.J. ("The Anti-Marcionite Prologues," *ThSt,* VII [1946], 393–409) denied the identity of authorship of the three Prologues and found no reason to date the Prologue to John before 300. See also B. W. Bacon, "The Latin Prologues of John," *JBL,* XXXII (1913), 194–212; "Marcion, Papias, and 'The Elders,'" *JTS,* XXIII (1921–22), 134–160; "The Anti-Marcionite Prologue to John," *JBL,* XLIX (1930), 43–54; and R. M. Grant, "The Oldest Gospel Prologues," *ATR,* XXIII (1941), 231–245 (who gives the text, translation, and commentary).

(3) The Muratorian Canon. Scholars have continued to debate the date, authorship, and literary character of this anonymous fragment. The view of Lightfoot, that its author was Hippolytus, was supported, with additional arguments, by T. H. Robinson (*Exp.,* Seventh Series, II [1906], 481–495), T. Zahn (*NKZ* XXXIII [1922], 417–436), M. J. Lagrange (*RB,* XXXV [1926], 83–88; and XLII [1933], 161–186). On the other hand, V. Bartlet thought Melito was its author (*Exp.,* Seventh Series, II [1906], 210–224); C. Erbes attributed it to Rhodon, who drew it up about A.D. 220 (*ZKG,* XXXV [1914], 331–362); and J. Chapman argued that it was part of Clement of Alexandria's *Hypotyposes* (*RBén,* XXI [1904], 240–264; see also 369–374 and XXII [1905], 62–64). Harnack maintained that it was an official list intended for the whole church, very probably of Roman origin with the authority of either Pope Victor or Pope Zephyrinus behind it (*ZNTW,* XXIV [1925], 1–16; cf. H. Koch's article condemning Harnack's reasoning but supporting his conclusions, *ZNTW,* XXV [1926], 154–160).

On the puzzling reference (lines 3 f. of the Canon) to Luke and Paul, see E. Nestle (*ZNTW,* X [1911], 177) and E. Klostermann (*ZNTW,* XXII [1923], 308 f.).

For other treatments, see E. S. Buchanan, "The Codex Muratorianus," *JTS,* VIII (1907), 537–545; H. Lietzmann, ed., *Das muratorische Fragment* (*KIT,* no. 1) (1902, 4th ed., 1933; reprinted by F. W. Grosheide in *Some Early Lists of the Books of the New Testament,* Leiden, 1948); A. Donini, "Il canone muratoriano," *Ricerche religiose,* II (1926), 127–138; S. Ritter, "Il frammento muratoriano," *Rivista di archeologia cristiana,* III (1926), 215–268; H. Leclercq, "Muratorianum," *DACL,* XII, 1 (1935), cols. 543-560 (with facsimile of the manuscript).

(4) The Priscillianist (or Monarchian) Prologues. These Latin Prologues, previously termed Monarchian and dated during the pontificate of Zephyrinus, A.D. 198–217 (so Corssen, *TU,* XV, 1, 1896), may be the work of either the Spanish heretic Priscillian of the latter part of the fourth century (so John Chapman, *Notes on the Early History of the Vulgate Gospels* [1908], pp. 217–288), or Instantius who defended Priscillian at the Council of Bordeaux in A.D. 384–385 (so G. Morin, *RBén* [1913], 153–173). These Prologues, having been reworked in an orthodox interest, were held in such high repute that they were incorporated in the Vulgate. H.

Lietzmann edited the Monarchian Prologues in his *KlT* series, no. 1, 1902, 4th ed., 1933. See also Gutwenger, *ThSt,* VII (1946), 403 ff.

(5) A Latin Version of the Eighty-fifth Apostolic Canon. C. H. Turner discovered (*JTS,* XIII [1912], 511–514) a Latin manuscript (Verona 51, fifth or sixth century) containing the Eighty-fifth Apostolic Canon (which concludes the eighth book of the Apostolic Constitutions), which presents a different list of New Testament books from that preserved in the Greek form of this Apostolic Canon. The Greek text, it should be noted, rests on manuscripts which are later by some centuries than this Latin manuscript. After enumerating by name the four Gospels and grouping the fourteen Epistles of Paul in one item, the list proceeds, "one Epistle of Peter, one Epistle of John, two Epistles of Clement, and these present constitutions . . . and the Acts of us the Apostles." Turner concludes, "At a rather later date than the *Apostolic Constitutions,* the Peshitta still knows only of three Catholic Epistles, I Peter, I John, and James; and I do not doubt that more critical texts of our fourth century authorities will tend to show that the full canon of seven Catholic Epistles only attained recognition at a later date than has hitherto been supposed" (*op. cit.,* p. 512).

(6) The Decretum Gelasianum. This document was previously thought to be an official statement, containing a list of canonical books, which embodied the decrees of the Council of 382 held at Rome under Pope Damasus. As the result of E. von Dobschuetz's research, however, it is now regarded as the private work of a cleric in Italy during the first half of the sixth century (Dobschuetz, *Das Decretum Gelasianum,* 1912; see also E. Schwartz, *ZNTW,* XXIX [1930], 161–168).

J. Chapman made an unsuccessful attempt to defend the traditional view of the Decretum (*RBén* [1913], 187–207, 315–333; cf. Amann in *RB* [1913], 602–608).

(7) A New Stichometrical List. C. H. Turner edited "An Unpublished Stichometrical List from the Freisingen MS of Canons" (*JTS,* II [1900–1], 236–253), in a manuscript of the eighth century, in which the epithet "canonical" is applied to the seven Catholic Epistles, and the title "Zelotes" is applied to Jude. This last agrees with the statement in the so-called Decretum Gelasianum, with Matt. 10:3 in certain Old Latin manuscripts, and with the mosaics of the great Baptistry at Ravenna.

(8) The Canon in the Syrian Church. The statement of Zahn (*Schaff-Herzog,* II, 398) that "Ephraem was familiar with all the Catholic epistles" (a view held also by J. A. Bewer, *The History of the New Testament Canon in the Syrian Church,* 1900 [reprinted from *AJT,* IV (1900), 64–98, 345–363]) goes beyond the reliable evidence so far as the Minor Catholic Epistles are concerned (Walter Bauer, *Der Apostolos der Syrer* [1903], pp. 40–53).

Three pieces of evidence have come to light bearing upon the canon of the Nestorian Church. Two corroborate the consensus of testimony that the Nestorian canon lacked II Peter, II and III John, Jude, and Revelation. (a) An anonymous Arabic chronicle of the ninth or tenth century testifies that the Babylonian Nestorians maintained their canon of twenty-two books (G. Rothstein, *ZDMG,* LVIII [1904], 634–663, 700–779). (b) An Arabic circular letter of A.D. 821 lists the New Testament books accepted by Nestorians as the four Gospels, Acts, and fourteen epistles of Paul (L. Rost, *ZNTW,* XXVII [1928], 103–196). Apparently opposed to this evidence is the testimony of the famous Nestorian monument erected A.D. 781 at Hsian-fu, China, which speaks of "the twenty-seven standard works of His [Christ's] Sutras" (Saeki's translation). In spite of its contradiction of all that is known elsewhere of the Nestorian canon, most scholars have felt that this must be interpreted as referring to the twenty-seven books of the New Testament. Sten Bugge, however, disputes the legitimacy of this interpretation, pointing out, *inter alia,* that nothing in the inscription alludes directly to *canonical* books ("Den syriske kirkes nytestamentlige kanon i China," *NTT,* XLI [1940], 97–118). On the monument in general, see P. Carus, *The Nestorian Monument,* 1909; P. Y. Saeki, *The Nestorian Monument in China,* 1916; A. C. Moule, *Christians in China Before the Year 1550,* 1930; W. Gummell's new translation of the Chinese text in Glasgow Oriental University Society, *Transactions,* VII (1934–35), 28–39; P. Y. Saeki, *The Nestorian Documents and Relics in China,* 1937; Gerhard Rosenkranz, *Die aelteste Christenheit in China,* 1938.

For information regarding the four Minor Catholic epistles and Revelation in the Philoxenian Syriac version, see John Gwynn, *The Apocalypse of St. John,* 1898, and *Remnants of the Later Syrian Versions of the Bible,* 1909.

In a hagiographical Syriac manuscript of A.D. 875, now in the British Museum (Wright, *Catalogue,* p. 1105), there is the statement that "in one of the villages of the Samaritans . . . those of the heresy of the Herodians . . . receive only Mark the Evangelist and three letters of Paul and four books of Moses . . ." (F. Nau, "Le canon biblique samaritano-chrétien des Hérodiens," *RB,* XXXIX [1930], 396–400).

B. APOCRYPHAL BOOKS: Only those apocryphal books are mentioned here for which serious claims to canonicity were made in the early church; for others, see APOCRYPHA, N.T. English translations, with brief introductions, are available in M. R. James, ed., *The Apocryphal New Testament,* 1924. See also E. J. Goodspeed, *Strange New Gospels,* 1931 (deals with modern forgeries), and K. L. Schmidt, *Kanonische und apokryphe Evangelien und Apostelgeschichten,* 1944.

(1) The Acts of Paul. Carl Schmidt's publication (*Acta Pauli,* 1936) of eleven pages of a Greek papyrus codex, written about A.D. 300, supplies a major portion hitherto lacking of this second-century apocryphon. One of the episodes in the papyrus tells of Paul's fighting wild beasts in the arena at Ephesus; the lion which is let loose on him, however, proves to be the same one which had previously been converted and baptized as the result of Paul's preaching (for translation and discussion, see B. M. Metzger, "St. Paul and the Baptized Lion," *Princeton Seminary Bulletin,* XXXIX, 2 [1945], 11–21). See also Rosa Soeder, *Die apokryphen Apostelgeschichten und die romanhafte Literatur der Antike,* 1932.

(2) Paul's Third Epistle to the Corinthians. This document, which for some time enjoyed canonical status in Syrian and Armenian churches, is contained in the apocryphal Acts of Paul. It deals with the status of early Christian prophets, the birth of Christ from the Virgin Mary, the human nature of Christ, and the resurrection of the flesh. See L. Vouaux, *Les actes de Paul et ses lettres apocryphes,* 1913; B. Pick, *IJA* (January, 1913), 9–13; and K. Pink, *Biblica,* VI (1925), 68–91. A. von Harnack edited the Epistle in Lietzmann's *Kleine Texte* series, No. 12, 2nd ed., 1931, and De Bruyne (*RBén,* XLV [1933], 189–195) and H. Boese (*ZNTW,* XLIV [1952–53], 66–76) published additional manuscripts containing the apocryphon.

(3) The Epistle to the Laodiceans. Several additional Latin manuscripts containing this apocryphon were edited by E. J. Goodspeed (*JBL,* XXIII [1904], 76–78; *AJT,* VIII [1904], 536–538). Harnack's idea (*SBA* [1923], 235–245) that this Epistle was a Marcionite forgery of the second half of the second century has not commended itself to other scholars. The most convenient edition is by Harnack in Lietzmann's *KlT* series, No. 12, 2nd ed., 1931. See also B. Pick, *IJA* (October, 1912), 73–76; and K. Pink, *Biblica,* VI (1925), 179–192.

(4) The Apocalypse of Peter. The complete text of the Ethiopic version of this book, held in high esteem by some in the early church, was published in 1910 (S. Grébaut, *ROC,* XV [1910], 198 ff., 307 ff., 425 ff.). Dating from the second century (it is mentioned in the Muratorian Canon), this Apocalypse continued to be used in the Liturgy of Good Friday in some churches of Palestine (Sozomen, *Hist. Eccl.,* vii, 19). It consists mainly of visions describing the beauty of heaven and the torments of hell. A later Arabic version was published by A. Mingana (*Woodbrooke Studies,* III, 2, 1931).

C. THE INFLUENCE OF ROLL AND CODEX ON COLLECTIONS OF NEW TESTAMENT BOOKS: The maximum length of a scroll convenient to handle (approximately thirty-one to thirty-two feet) could contain the equivalent of either the Gospel of Luke or Acts. As long as Christians used the roll in the transmission of their sacred books, the four Gospels or the Pauline Epistles could be collected in an external way only by assembling several rolls in the same box or chest (*capsa;* cf. *Acts of Scillitan Martyrs,* A.D. 180, for evidence regarding Paul's Epistles). When, however, the codex or leaf-form of books was adopted, many or even all the separate documents of the New Testament could be more closely assembled in one book.

Evidence recently collected shows that the Christians made almost exclusive use of the codex form for the transmission of their Scriptures at a much earlier date than was heretofore thought probable (C. H. Roberts, "The Christian Book and the Greek Papyri," *JTS,* L [1949], 155–168). It has been suggested (Roberts, *JTS,* XL [1939], 257; elaborated by Peter Katz, *JTS,* XLVI [1945], 63–65) that the Gentile Christian church, in opposition to the Synagogue, may have deliberately substituted the codex for the traditional Jewish scroll. However this may be, considerations of economy (using both sides of the writing material) and ease in the consultation of proof-texts would certainly have encouraged Christians to adopt this format for their sacred books. See also Hugo Ibscher, "Der Kodex," *Buch und Schrift, Jahrbuch der Einbandkunst,* X (1937), 3–15; W. Schubart, "Das antike Buch," *Die Antike,* XIV (1938), 171–195.

D. PROBLEMS REGARDING THE CANON: Although the recognition of the canon of the New Testament was one of the most important developments in the early church, there is a surprising absence of contemporary references to (1) the order in which the various parts of the New Testament achieved general currency, and (2) the reasons which led the church to make the selection that ultimately prevailed. The following are some representative theories on both these matters.

(1) Harnack held that the Gospels were the nucleus of the canon, and that the Pauline Epistles followed. The Acts of the Apostles was added chiefly to vindicate the authority of Paul and to join his writings to the Gospels (for a sharp critique, see H. C. Vedder, "The Origin of the New Testament," *The Union Seminary Review* (Richmond), XXXVIII [1926–27], 146–158).

According to E. J. Goodspeed the first collection of New Testament books was made by a Christian, perhaps at Ephesus, whose interest in Paul had been roused by reading the recently published Acts of the Apostles (shortly after A.D. 90). This admirer of the Apostle composed a prefatory encyclical (Ephesians) and published the corpus of ten letters (i.e., all but the Pastorals), which in turn called forth the composition of other letters, namely Rev. 1–3, Hebrews, I Peter, and I Clement. See, among several publications where Goodspeed advanced these theories, his *New Solutions of the New Testament Problems* (1927), and "The Editio Princeps of Paul," *JBL*, LXIV (1945), 193–204; cf. A. E. Barnett, *Paul Becomes a Literary Influence,* 1941. John Knox conjectured that the collector and publisher of the preliminary Pauline corpus was Onesimus (*Philemon among the Letters of Paul,* 1935).

Hans Windisch thought that the Book of Revelation, because it contained words of Jesus Christ, history of the Kingdom, and letters, supplied the pattern for the canonization of documents in each of these three areas ("Der Apokalyptiker Johannes als Begruender des neutestamentlichen Kanons," *ZNTW,* X [1909], 148–174).

The question whether the church's canon preceded or followed Marcion's canon continues to be debated, but in view of the consistent representation in the Fathers that Marcion *rejected* certain books, the great probability is that the church's canon was anterior to Marcion's rival canon (so C. H. Turner, *JTS,* X, 357 f.; J. Chapman, *RBén,* XXIX [1912], 252; J. Moffatt, *Introduction to the New Testament,* p. 60; E. C. Blackman, *Marcion and His Influence* [1948], p. 32).

John Knox proposed the elaborate hypothesis that Marcion had a kind of proto-Luke which the church later enlarged in the interest of anti-Marcionite polemic, producing our present Luke sometime after A.D. 150 (*Marcion and the New Testament, An Essay in the Early History of the Canon,* 1942). Knox fails, however, to show that after A.D. 150 conditions prevailed in the church to render possible the immediate general acceptance of a newly redacted Gospel (see also C. Kraeling, *CQ,* XX [1943], 159–161).

Taking up a suggestion made by J. Chapman ("The Earliest New Testament," *Exp.,* Sixth Series, XII [1905], 119–127), J. H. Ropes hazarded the theory that the formation of the basic canon took place early in the second century, perhaps at Antioch. The "Western" text (found today in such manuscripts as Codex Bezae, the Old Latin manuscripts, and other witnesses) "was the text of the primitive 'canon' (if the term may be pardoned in referring to so early a date), and was expressly created for that purpose" (Ropes, *The Text of Acts* [1926], p. ix). Later the "Western" text was "supplanted by a 'pre-canonical' text of superior age and merit [i.e., the Neutral or Alexandrian or Old Uncial]" (*ibid.,* p. ccxlv).

(2) Various answers have been given to the question why the church approved certain books and rejected others. According to Harnack, the canon constituted one of the three barriers (the other two were the creed and the bishops) which the church erected in its struggle with heresy, particularly Gnosticism. The process involved essentially the competition of many and the survival of the fittest. Juelicher, on the other hand, stressed the importance of *anagnosis,* or "[public] reading," of New Testament documents along with Old Testament documents, already regarded as canonical, with the consequent impartation of the authority of the latter to the former. Conflict, so far from decreasing the canonical material by selection, actually worked to increase the amount subsequently canonized by widening the church's acquaintance of acceptable literature. According to Westcott, the formation of the canon was among the first instinctive acts of the Christian society, resting upon the general confession of the churches and not upon the independent opinions of its members. The canon was not the result of a series of contests; rather, canonical books were separated from the others by the intuitive insight of the church.

E. THE THEOLOGY OF THE CANON: Discussion of the canon should distinguish between the ground of canonicity and the grounds of the conviction of canonicity. The latter were variously apprehended in different parts of the ancient church. In some areas (e.g., Alexandria) the process of canonization proceeded by way of selection, moving from many to few; in other areas (e.g., Syria) the church was content with a canon of twenty-two books. The ground of canonicity, on the other hand, rests ultimately upon what God has accomplished through Christ and the Spirit. Luther recognized as canonical those writings which preach Christ. (For a systematic treatment from this point of view, see Martin Albertz, *Botschaft des Neuen Testamentes,* I, ii, *Die Entstehung des apostolischen Schriftkanons,* 1952.) Calvin defined the authority of the Scriptures in terms of the activity of God's Spirit (*testimonium Spiritus Sancti internum*). According to a modern Reformed theologian, "The concept of the canon is bound up with the concept of God. . . . God is *ho kanōn*" (F. W. Grosheide, *Algemeene canoniek van het Nieuwe Testament* [1935], pp. 9 f.). In this sense, the church did not create the canon, but came to recognize and acknowledge the self-authenticating quality of the canonical documents, which imposed themselves as such upon the church.

BIBLIOGRAPHY: In addition to works mentioned above: I. Guidi, "Il canone biblico della chiesa copta," *Revue Biblique,* X (1901), 161–174; E. C. Moore, *The New Testament in the Christian Church,* 1904; Paul Ewald, *Der Kanon des Neuen Testaments,* 1906; Hans Lietzmann, *Wie wurden die Buecher des Neuen Testaments heilige Schrift?,* 1907; U. Fracassini, "Le origini del canone del N.T.," *Rivista storica-critica,* IV (1908), 349–368, 433–445; R. H. Gruetzmacher, "Die Haltbarkeit des Kanonbegriffes," *Theol. Studien. Th. Zahn dargebracht* (1908), pp. 47–68; Johannes Leipoldt, *Geschichte des neutestamentlichen Kanons;* II, *Mittelalter und Neuzeit,* 1908; Henry C. Vedder, *Our New Testament: How Did We Get it?,* 1908; C. H. Turner, "The Growth of the Idea of the Canon of the New Testament," *JTS,* X (1909), 13 ff.,

160 ff., 354 ff.; E. Jacquier, *Le Nouveau Testament dans l'église chrétienne; I, Préparation, formation et définition du canon du Nouveau Testament,* 3rd ed., 1911; P. Dausch, *Der Kanon des Neuen Testaments,* 1910, 4th ed., 1921; G. F. Moore, "The Definition of the Jewish Canon and the Repudiation of Christian Scriptures," *Essays in Modern Theology and Related Subjects . . . A Testimonial to C. A. Briggs* (1911), pp. 99–125; Alexander Souter, *The Text and Canon of the New Testament,* 1913; A. von Harnack, *Die Entstehung des Neuen Testaments und die wichtigsten Folgen der neuen Schoepfung,* 1914; Eng. tr., *The Origin of the New Testament and the Most Important Consequences,* 1925; E. von Dobschuetz, "The Abandonment of the Canonical Idea," *AJT,* XIX (1915), 416–429; I. Haenel, *Der Schriftbegriff Jesu. Studie zur Kanongeschichte,* 1917; Ed. Koenig, *Kanon und Apokryphen,* 1917; A. Fridrichsen, *Den nytestamentlige skriftsamlings historie,* 1918; W. S. Reilly, "Le canon du N.T. et le critère de la canonicité," *Revue Biblique,* XXX (1921), 195–205; Sigurd Odland, *Det nytestamentlige Kanon,* 1922; Johannes Bestmann, *Zur Geschichte den neutestamentlichen Kanons,* 1922; E. J. Goodspeed, *The Formation of the New Testament,* 1926; H. Hoepfl, "Canonicité," *Dictionnaire de la Bible, Supplément,* I (1928), cols. 1022–1045; Albert Maichle, *Der Kanon der biblischen Buecher und das Konzil von Trient,* 1929; N. B. Stonehouse, *The Apocalypse in the Ancient Church,* 1929; G. M. Perrella, *De apostolico et prophetico munere et inspirationis et canonicitatis criterio altero pro N. altero pro V.T.,* 1931; M. J. Lagrange, *Histoire ancienne du canon Nouveau Testament,* 1933; H. Strathmann, *Die Entstehung des Neuen Testaments,* 1936; H. Oppel, *Kanōn,* 1937; S. M. Zarb, *Il canone biblico,* 1937; J. Brinktrine, "Nach welchen Gesichtspunkten wurden die einzelnen Gruppen des neutestamentlichen Kanons geordnet?" *Biblische Zeitschrift,* XXIV (1938–39), 125–135; D. W. Riddle, "Factors in the Formation of the New Testament Canon," *Journal of Religion,* XIX (1939), 330–345; O. Cullmann, "Die Pluralitaet der Evangelien als theologisches Problem im Altertum," *Theologische Zeitschrift,* I (1945), 23–42; T. W. Manson, "The Johannine Epistles and the Canon of the New Testament," *JTS,* XLVIII (1947), 32–33; A. C. Cotter, "Lost Books of the Bible?" *Theological Studies,* VI (1945), 206–228; Olaf Moe, "Hebreerbrevets betydning innenfor den nytestamentlige kanon," *Korsets ord og troens tale, Festskrift til . . . O. Hallesby* (1949), pp. 92–102; W. C. van Unnik, "De la règle *mēte prostheinai mēte aphelein* dans l'histoire du canon," *VC,* III (1949), 1–36; W. C. Kuemmel, "Notwendigkeit und Grenze des neutestamentlichen Kanons," *Zeitschrift fuer Theologie und Kirche,* XLVII (1950), 277–313.

Many handbooks on introduction to the New Testament have sections dealing with the canon. Special studies on the canon in ecclesiastical writers (arranged in chronological order) include the following: *The New Testament in the Apostolic Fathers,* edited by a Committee of the Oxford Society of Historical Theology, 1905; Aguado Esteban, "San Teófilo de Antioquía y el canon del N.T.," *E.B.,* VI (1934), 290–326; A. Camerbynk, *Saint Irénée et la canon du N.T.,* 1896; J. Hoh, *Die Lehre des hl. Irenaeus ueber das N.T.* (*Neutestamentliche Abhandlungen,* VII), 1919; H. Kutter, *Klemens Alexandrinus und das N.T.,* 1897; P. Dausch, *Der neutestamentliche Schriftkanon und Klemens von Alexandrien,* 1899; J. Ruwet, "Les 'antilegomena' dans les oeuvres d'Origène," *Biblica,* XXIII (1942), 18–42; XXIV (1943), 18–58; XXV (1944), 311–334; *idem,* "Le canon alexandrin des écritures, Saint Athanase," *Biblica,* XXXIII (1952), 1–29; T. Zahn, *Athanasius und der Bibelkanon,* 1901; *idem,* "Das N.T. Theodors von Mopsuestia und der urspruengliche Kanon der Syrer," *NKZ,* XI (1900), 788–806; C. Baur, "Der Kanon des hl. Joh. Chrysostomus," *TQ,* CV (1924), 258–271 (of about 11,000 citations from the N.T., there is none from II Pet., II and III Jn, Jude. and Rev.); V. Tzortzatos, *Hē peri tōn hagiōn graphōn didaskalia tou Chrysostomou,* Athens, 1947; H. H. Howorth, "The Influence of St. Jerome on the Canon of the Western Church," *JTS,* X (1909), 481–496; XI (1910), 321–347; XIII (1912), 1–18; C. J. Costello, *St. Augustine's Doctrine on the Inspiration and Canonicity of Scripture,* 1930; *idem,* "St. Augustine's Canon of Scripture and His Criterion of Canonicity," *Revue de l'Université d'Ottawa* (1932), pp. 125*–138*; A. Tapia Basulto, "El canon escriturístico en S. Isidore de Savilla," *Ciencia Tomista,* LVIII (1939), 364–388; C. van der Borne, "De canone biblico S. Bonaventurae," *Archiv franc. hist.,* XVIII (1925), 313–317; P. Synave, "Le canon scripturaire de Saint Thomas d'Aquin," *RB,* XXXIII (1924), 522–533; H. H. Howorth, "The Origin and Authority of the Biblical Canon According to the Continental Reformers," *JTS,* VIII (1907), 321–365; IX (1908), 188–230; X (1909), 183–232; *idem,* "The Bible Canon of the Reformers," *IJA* (October, 1913), pp. 66–70; A. Maichle, *Der Kanon der biblischen Buecher und das Konzil von Trient* (*Freiburger theologische Studien,* XXXIII), 1929; H. H. Howorth, "The Origin and Authority of the Biblical Canon in the Anglican Church," *JTS,* VIII (1907), 1–40.

[Sup.] Bruce M. Metzger.

THE PRINCIPAL VERSIONS OF THE BIBLE

VI

BIBLE VERSIONS: The versions dealt with in this article are divided into two principal groups, ancient and modern. The ancient versions include all the known versions produced down to the close of the tenth Christian century; so far as practicable these are arranged in approximate chronological order. The modern versions include those of the principal languages of Europe and America, arranged in alphabetical order. These are concluded with a cross reference to an article which treats Bible versions on the mission field.

In addition to the special bibliographies supplied for individual versions, the following books are of general importance.

T. H. Darlow and H. F. Moule, *Historical Catalogue of the Printed Editions of Holy Scripture in the Library of the British and Foreign Bible Society* (2 vols., 1903–8); R. Kilgour, *The Gospel in Many Years* (1929); O. M. Norlie, *The Bible in a Thousand Tongues* (1935); British Museum, *General Catalogue of Printed Books,* Vols. XVI-XVIII (1936–37); Eric M. North, *The Book of a Thousand Tongues* (1938); R. Kilgour, *The Bible Throughout the World* (1939); F. G. Kenyon, *Our Bible and the Ancient Manuscripts,* (4th ed., 1939); H. W. Robinson (ed.), *The Bible in Its Ancient and English Versions* (1941); Ira M. Price, *The Ancestry of Our English Bible* (2nd rev. ed., by W. A. Irwin and A. P. Wikgren, 1949; corrected ed., 1951); B. M. Metzger, "The Evidence of the Versions for the Text of the New Testament," in M. M. Parvis and A. P. Wikgren (eds.), *New Testament Manuscript Studies* (1950), pp. 25–68 and 177–208; Bleddyn J. Roberts, *The Old Testament Text and Versions* (1951); B. M. Metzger, *Annotated Bibliography of the Textual Criticism of the New Testament* (1955), pp. 27–65; Arthur Vööbus, *Early Versions of the New Testament, Manuscript Studies* (*Papers of the Estonian Theological Society in Exile,* No. 6, 1954).

I. Ancient Versions:

A. THE SEPTUAGINT: See article, SEPTUAGINT, THE.

B. LATIN VERSIONS: 1. THE LATIN BIBLE BEFORE JEROME: The suggestion by several scholars (e.g., D. S. Blondheim, *Les parlers judéo-romans et la Vetus Latina,* 1925; A. Baumstark, *ZDMG,* N.F. XIV, 89–118), that alleged Semitic influence upon the Old Latin translations of the Old Testament indicates that they were made originally from the Hebrew or the Aramaic Targums, has not been accepted by most investigators, who continue to hold that Christians made the version from the Septuagint. Despite others' assertions that the Old Latin of the Old Testament is markedly "Lucianic," J. A. Montgomery found no evidence of characteristic Lucianic doublets in Daniel (*Commentary,* pp. 45–46). On the other hand, his analyses corroborated Burkitt's dictum that Old Latin citations by the fathers are distinctly pre-Hexaplaric. Among suggestions as to the place of origin of the Old Latin (North Africa, Antioch in Syria, and Rome), the most recent research points to Rome (G. Bardy, *La question des langues dans l'église ancienne,* I, 1948; Christine Mohrmann, "Les origines de la latinité chrétienne à Rome," *VC,* III, [1949], 67–106, and 163–183). Besides the two main types of pre-Jerome Latin translations (African and European), traces of another, much nearer the Septuagint, are to be found in quotations by Augustine (Burkitt in *JTS,* XI, [1910], 258–268).

In the New Testament the textual complexion of the Old Latin is typically Western, and as a rule the African form offers the larger divergencies, the European the smaller. The remarkable variations among the Old Latin manuscripts may perhaps be explained on the supposition that the scribes regarded their work not in terms of mechanical transmission, but as producing a "Targum" which incorporated their own and others' traditions. That is to say, the Old Latin was a living creation constantly growing even after the publication of Jerome's Vulgate (see Montgomery, *Daniel,* p. 45; von Soden in Juelicher's *Festgabe* [1927], p. 273; H. H. Glunz, *History of the Vulgate in England* [1933], pp. 14 ff.).

Three important series of publications of Old Latin evidence are in the course of production: A. Juelicher's edition of the *Itala; Das Neue Testament in altlateinischer Ueberlieferung nach den Handschriften,* I: *Matthaeus* (1938); II: *Markus* (1940); III: *Lukas* (1955); and the Benedictine *Vetus Latina; Die Reste der altlateinischen Bibel nach Petrus Sabatier neugesammelt und herausgegeben von der Erzabtei Beuron,* of which there have been published *Verzeichnis der Sigel* (1948), and the first part of *Genesis* (ed. B. Fischer, 1951); and Teófilo Ayuso, *La Vetus Latina Hispana;* I: *Prolegómenos* (1953).

BIBLIOGRAPHY: Old Testament: A. Amelli, *Liber Psalmorum juxta antiquissimum latinam versionem,* Rome, 1912; P. (later Bernard) Capelle, *Le texte du psautier latin en Afrique,* 1913; A. Dold, *Konstanzer altlateinische Propheten und Evangelienbruchstuecke,* 1923 (26 folios of Ezekiel, Daniel, and Minor Prophets); A. V. Billen, *The Old Latin Texts of the Heptateuch,* 1927; A. Allgeier, *Die altlateinische Psalterien,* 1928; B. Motzo, *La versione latina di Ester secondo i LXX,* 1928; A. Allgeier, "Das afrikanisches Element im althispanischen Psalter," *Spanische Forschungen,* II (1930), 196–228; H. Degering and A. Boeckler, *Die Quedlinburger Itala Fragmenta,* Berlin, 1932 (new fragments of Samuel and Kings); D. De Bruyne, "Les plus anciennes versions latines du Cantique," *R. Bén*, XXXVIII (1926), 97–115; A. Dold, *Neue St. Galler vorhieronymische Propheten-Fragmenta*, 1940; J. Schildenberger, *Die altlateinische Texte des Proverbienbuches*, 1941; R. Weber, *Les plus anciennes versions latines du IIe livre des Paralipomènes*, 1945; B. Bischoff, "Neue Materialien zum Bestand und zur Geschichte der altlateinischen Bibeluebersetzungen," *Miscellanea G. Mercati*, I (1947), 410 ff.

New Testament: A. Reichardt, *Der Codex Boernerianus der Briefe des Apostel Paulus*, 1909; E. S. Buchanan, *The Four Gospels from the Codex Veronensis*, 1911; H. J. Vogels, *Codex Rehdigeranus. Die vier Evangelien nach der lateinischen Handschrift 169 der Stadtbibliothek Breslau*, 1913; C. Cipolla, *Il codice evangelico "k" della biblioteca universitaria di Torino*, 1913; A. Gasquet, *Codex Vercellensis*, Rome, 1914; A. Juelicher, "Kritische Analyse der lateinischen Uebersetzungen der Apostelgeschichte," *ZNTW*, XV (1914), 163–188; H. J. Vogels, *Untersuchungen zur Geschichte der lateinischen Apokalypsenuebersetzungen*, 1920; C. H. Milne, *A Reconstruction of the Old Latin Text or Texts of the Gospels Used by St. Augustine*, 1926; H. J. Vogels, *Evangelium Palatinum, Studien zur aeltesten Geschichte der lateinischen Evangelienuebersetzung*, 1926; A. Bakker, *A Full Collation of Codex Evang. Bobbiensis (k)*, 1933; G. Godu, *Codex Sarzanensis, fragments d'ancienne version latine du quatrième évangile*, 1936; T. Ayuso Marazuela, "Una importante colección de notas marginales de la Vetus Latina Hispana," *EB*, IX (1950), 328–378.

On the linguistic phenomena of the Old Latin (besides Blondheim's work cited above), see A. Allgeier, "Vergleichende Untersuchungen zum Sprachgebrauch der lateinischen Uebersetzungen der Psalmen und der Evangelien," *ZATW*, XLVI (1928) 34–49; P. W. Hoogterp, *Étude sur le latin du Codex Bobbiensis (k) des évangiles*, 1930; W. Suess, *Studien zur lateinischen Bibel*, I: *Augustins locutiones und das Problem der lateinischen Bibelsprache*, 1932; W. Matzkow, *De vocabulis quibusdam Italae et Vulgatae christianis quaestiones lexicographicae*, Berlin, 1933; Robert C. Stone, *The Language of the Latin Text of Codex Bezae*, 1946.

2. THE LATIN VULGATE: The Vulgate text of the Old Testament is far from being uniform; in the historical books Jerome's skill and originality as translator of the Hebrew are most conspicuous, whereas in the Prophets and Psalter he often deliberately accepted the rendering of the Greek versions (cf. F. Stummer, *Einfuehrung in die lateinischen Bibel* [1928], pp. 99–110). Contrary to A. Condamin's denial of the influence of Jewish tradition on Jerome (*RSR*, V [1914], 1–21), C. H. Gordon found ample evidence in Proverbs to substantiate the generally accepted view that Jerome frequently followed current Rabbinical interpretations (*JBL*, XLIX [1930], 384–416). With regard to Jerome's revisions of the Psalter, De Bruyne maintained that the so-called *Psalterium Romanum* is not the work of Jerome (whose revision made for Pope Damasus has been lost), but is an Old Latin Psalter erroneously attributed to Jerome (*R. Bén.*, XLII [1930], 447–482). This was refuted by A. Allgeier, who, inverting the sequence customarily proposed for Jerome's three revisions of the Psalter, held that the first was *Psalterium iuxta Hebraeos*, the second *Psalterium Gallicanum* (both based on the Hexaplaric Greek text of Origen), and the third *Psalterium Romanum* (A. Allgeier, *Die altlateinischen Psalterien*, 1928; and *Die Psalmen der Vulgata*, 1940).

The Vulgate text of the New Testament poses many problems for the textual critic. No unanimity of opinion prevails as to the type of Greek text which Jerome chose as a standard by which to revise the Old Latin. Von Soden believed that it was like the archetype of his own three great recensions, *I*, *H*, and *K* (*Die Schriften des Neuen Testaments*, I, iii [1910], 1524–1532). Vogels maintained that in the Gospels Jerome utilized what is called the Koine type of Greek text (*Vulgatastudien* [1928], pp. 55–80). Burkitt, however, denied that Jerome consulted only one type of Greek text, and held that he depended on at least two, one similar to that found in codex Vaticanus, and the other similar to that found in codex Alexandrinus (*JTS*, XXX [1929], 408–412). Lagrange agreed with Burkitt in part, but thought that Jerome was influenced by the type of text represented by codex Sinaiticus even more than by that in codex Alexandrinus (*Critique textuelle* [1935], 287 ff.).

In the Acts Ropes found that the Vulgate agrees most often with codex Alexandrinus (*The Text of Acts* [1926], p. cxxvii).

De Bruyne proposed the startling thesis that what is commonly taken to be Jerome's Vulgate text of the Pauline Epistles is none other than the work of Pelagius (*Revue Biblique*, N.S. XII [1915], 358–392). Cavallera went still further and denied that Jerome had any part in making the Vulgate text of the Acts, Epistles, and Apocalypse (*Bulletin de littérature ecclésiastique* [1920], 269–292). Against these views the traditional opinion was upheld by Buonaiuti (*ET*, XXVII [1915–16], 425–427), Souter (*JTS*, XVI [1915], 105), Mangenot (*RB*, N.S. XV [1918], 244–253), and Chapman (*JTS*, XXIV [1923], 33–51).

For the Catholic Epistles of the Vulgate there exists a distinctive type of text of great importance for the textual critic (von Harnack, *Zur Revision der Principien der neutestamentlicher Textkritik*, 1916).

The most thorough study of Jerome's text of Revelation is that by Vogels, who found many resemblances of the Vulgate to codex Sinaiticus (*Untersuchungen zur Geschichte der lateinischen Apokalypsenuebersetzung*, 1920).

Several scholars have attempted to disentangle the complicated strands of national types of Vulgate text which emerged during the Middle Ages; e.g., Hans Glunz, *Britannien und Bibeltext, der Vulgatatext der Evangelien . . .* (1930); *idem*, *History of the Vulgate in England from Alcuin to Roger Bacon . . .* (1933); L. J. Hopkins-James, *The Celtic Gospels . . .* (1934); J. M. Bover, "La Vulgata en España," (*EB*, seg. época, I [1941–42], 11–40, 167–185; cf. VIII [1948], 161 f.).

In 1907 Pope Pius X appointed Abbot (later Cardinal) Gasquet, president of the English Benedictines, as head of a commission entrusted with the revision of the text of the Vulgate. The so-called *règle de fer* for evaluating variant readings, which Dom Henri Quentin elaborated for the textual criticism of the Vulgate (*Mémoire sur l'établissement du texte de la Vulgate*,

1922), was subjected to devastating criticism by E. K. Rand (*HTR,* XVII [1924], 197–264), Chapman (*R. Bén.,* XXXVII [1925], 5–40, 365–403), and Stummer (*ZATW,* N.F., IV [1927], 141–151). Thus far nine volumes have been published: Genesis (1926); Exodus, Leviticus (1929); Numbers, Deuteronomy (1936); Joshua, Judges, Ruth (1939); Samuel (1944); Kings (1945); Chronicles (1948); Ezra, Tobias, Judith (1950); Esther, Job (1951).

The edition of the New Testament, begun by Wordsworth and White in 1879, with the publication of Matthew in 1889, has now been completed by H. F. D. Sparks (1954).

Bibliography: F. Amann, *Die Vulgata Sixtina von 1590,* 1912; H. Hoepfl, *Beitraege zur Geschichte der Sixto-Klementinischen Vulgata,* 1913; A. Juelicher, "Kritische Analyse der lateinischen Uebersetzungen der Apostelgeschichte," *ZNTW,* XV (1914), 163–188; Ambrosius Amelli, *Cassiodoro e la Volgata,* 1917; J. M. Harden, *Psalterium iuxta Hebraeos Hieronymi,* 1922; Henri Quentin, *Essais de critique textuelle,* 1926; *idem, La Vulgate à travers les siècles et sa révision actuelle,* 1926; C. H. Turner, *The Oldest Manuscript of the Vulgate Gospels . . . ,* 1931; Alban Dold, *Zwei Bobbienser Palimpseste mit fruehestem Vulgatatext,* 1931; G. Sacco, *La Volgata latina e il testo del Nuovo Testament,* 1933; N. Greitemann, *De Windesheimse Vulgaatrevisie in de vijftiende Eeuw,* 1937; Pierre Salmon, *La révision de la Vulgate,* 1937; Hans Rost, *Die Bibel im Mittelalter,* 1939; J. Ziegler, *Die juengeren griechischen Uebersetzungen als Vorlagen der Vulgata in den prophetischen Schriften,* 1943–44; Jan O. Smit, *De Vulgaat,* 1948.

On the language of the Vulgate, see John J. Jepson, *The Latinity of the Vulgate Psalter,* 1915; W. E. Plater and H. J. White, *A Grammar of the Vulgate,* 1926; M. Stenzel, "Zum Wortschatz der NT Vulgata," *VC,* VI (1952), 20–27; as well as the studies listed at the close of the preceding bibliography on the Old Latin.

3. later latin translations: In 1529 there was published at Wittenberg a revision of part of the Latin Vulgate, made by unknown translator(s)—Luther; Melanchthon; Bucer?—on the basis of the original texts and Luther's German version. It embraced only the Pentateuch, Joshua, Judges, the Books of Kings, and the New Testament. According to Eberhard Nestle, who edited the reprint for the Weimar edition of Luther's *Werke* (*Die Deutsche Bibel,* Vol. 5, 1914), in the New Testament the version frequently improves upon Jerome's Latinity and at the same time comes closer to the Greek text (Nestle in *Philologus,* LXXI [1912], 314–317).

In 1941 Pope Pius XII assigned to the Pontifical Biblical Institute in Rome the task of preparing a new Latin translation of the Psalms directly from the Hebrew. This *Liber Psalmorum* was completed in 1944, and a second edition with the seventeen canticles from the Old and New Testaments which are used in the Psalter of the Roman Breviary appeared in 1945. The translators sought to be faithful to the original while having a careful regard for "the venerable Vulgate" and other ancient versions (*Acta Apostolicae Sedis,* XXXVII [1945], 65–67). See also Augustinus Bea, *Il nuovo salterio latino* (2nd ed., 1946), also in French (1947) and German (1949) translations.

In 1950 Bea published his Latin translation of *Liber Ecclesiastae . . . qui ab Hebraeis appelatur Qohelet.*

Bibliography: For a discussion of Latin versions of the sixteenth century, see Hugh Pope, *English Versions of the Bible* (1952), 99–128.

C. SYRIAC VERSIONS: 1. the old syriac: Though Torrey has argued for Palestine as the origin of this version (*Documents of the Primitive Church* [1941], pp. 345–370), most scholars continue to regard Edessa as its birthplace. Vööbus' research has revealed the persistence of sporadic Old Syriac variants in ecclesiastical authors down to the twelfth century. From the form of quotations in Ephraem's commentaries on the Acts and Pauline Epistles, extant in Armenian, it appears that an older form of the Syriac text for these books preceded the Peshitta, even though no manuscript of this has survived (Conybeare in J. H. Ropes, *The Text of Acts* [1926], 373–453; Joseph Molitor, *Der Paulustext des hl. Ephraem . . . ,* 1938). See also Harmony of the Gospels (Tatian's).

2. the peshitta: The Peshitta of the Old Testament, at least in the Pentateuch, is thought to be of Jewish or Jewish Christian origin (J. Bloch, *AJSL,* XXXV [1919], 215–222; A. Baumstark, *Geschichte der syrischen Literatur* [1922], p. 18; R. H. Pfeiffer, *Introduction to the Old Testament* [1941], p. 120). Some books of the Old Testament, e.g., Genesis (Haenel), II Samuel (Englert), the Psalms (Berg), reveal influence from the Septuagint. Esther is a careful but not slavish rendering of the Hebrew. Chronicles has the paraphrastic characteristics of a Targum. Proverbs is free but, on the whole, faithful to the original (Pinkuss, *ZATW,* XIV [1894], 65–141; Chajes, *JQR,* XIII [1901], 86 ff.). Lamentations and Ezra follow the Masoretic text carefully (Abalesz; Hawley).

Whether Rabbula, Bishop of Edessa (411–435), made the Peshitta of the New Testament (so Burkitt and many following him), appears to be somewhat less certain in view of Vööbus' researches (yet see Matthew Black's critique in *Bulletin of the John Rylands Library,* XXXIII [1951], 203–210, and in *Bulletin* of *Studiorum Novi Testamenti Societas* [1950], 51–62). As to text type, Gwilliam found that, in Matt. 1–14, the Peshitta agrees with the *textus receptus* 108 times and with Vaticanus 65 times, while in 137 cases it differs from both, usually with the support of the Old Syriac or the Old Latin (*Studia Biblica et Ecclesiastica,* V [1903], 187–237). In Acts the Peshitta preserves many Old Syriac readings in a text substantially like that of the Old Uncials (J. H. Ropes, *The Text of Acts,* pp. 291–316).

3. the philoxenian and/or harclean syriac: The problem whether the Philoxenian Syriac version was reissued by Thomas of Heraclea or whether the second was an entirely new version has not yet been solved. In any case, the Harclean marginal variants in Acts are second

only to codex Bezae in importance for the Western text.

John Gwynn edited *The Apocalypse of John in a Syriac Version Hitherto Unknown* (being the first Syriac book issued from the Dublin University Press, 1897), which he identified as the Philoxenian version. He also edited *The Four Minor Catholic Epistles* (II Peter, II and III John, Jude) of the same version (1909). In the same volume there are included also the *pericope de adultera* (in two recensions) and fragments of the Syro-Hexaplar version of the Septuagint (Gen., Lev., I and II Chron., Neh.). Zuntz finds influence in the Harclean version from the Caesarean type of text, but the reliability of his work has been questioned by Kilpatrick and McHardy (*JTS,* XLVIII [1947], 92–99).

4. THE PALESTINIAN SYRIAC: The view commonly held is that the Pentateuch in this version was made from the Septuagint. Baumstark, however, maintained that it goes back to a Jewish Palestinian Pentateuch Targum (*OC,* 3te Serie, X, 201–224). In the Gospels the version appears to be a witness of the Caesarean text (so Lake-Blake-New, *HTR,* XXI [1928], 312–323). For literature down to 1924, see Friedrich Schulthess, *Grammatik des christlichpalaestinischen Aramaeisch* (1924). Additional fragments were published by Hugo Duensing, in *ZNTW,* XXXVII (1938), 42–46; Matthew Black, *Bulletin of the John Rylands Library,* XXIII (1939), 201–214; Duensing, *Nachrichten der Ak. der Wiss. in Goettingen,* phil.-hist. Kl. (1944); and Black, *A Christian Palestinian Syriac Horologion* (1954).

BIBLIOGRAPHY: J. F. Berg, *The Influence of the Septuagint on the Peshitta Psalter,* 1895; A. Abalesz, *Die syrische Uebersetzung der Klagelieder . . . ,* 1895; J. Haenel, *Die aussermasoretischen Uebereinstimmungen zwischen der Septuaginta und der Peschitta in der Genesis,* 1911; C. A. Hawley, *A Critical Examination of the Peshitta Version of the Book of Ezra,* 1922; M. J. Wyngarden, *The Syriac Version of the Book of Daniel,* 1923; Leo Haefeli, *Die Peschitta des Alten Testaments mit Rucksicht auf ihre textkritische Bearbeitung und Herausgabe,* 1927; C. Moss, "The Peshitta Version of Ezra," *Le Muséon,* XLVI (1933), 58–110; Franz Rosenthal, *Die aramaistische Forchung seit Th. Noeldeke's Veroeffentlichungen,* 1939; P. A. H. de Boer, *Research into the Text of I Samuel I-XVI* (1938), pp. 22–43; Guenther Zuntz, *The Ancestry of the Harklean New Testament,* 1945; J. van der Ploeg, "Recente Pesitta-Studies (sinds 1927)," *Jaarbericht van het Vooraziatisch-Egyptisch Gezelschap, Ex Oriente Lux,* X (1948), 392–399; Donald M. C. Englert, *The Peshitto of Second Samuel,* 1949; Arthur Vööbus, *Studies in the History of the Gospel Text in Syriac,* 1951; A. Vogel, "Studien zum Peschitta-Psalter," *Biblica,* XXXII (1951), 32–56, 198–231, 336–363, 481–502.

D. THE SAMARITAN PENTATEUCH: This text (which, being Hebrew written in Samaritan characters, is not strictly a version) differs from the Masoretic text in about 6,000 places, in more than 1,900 of which it agrees with the Septuagint (Kahle in *Theologische Studien und Kritiken,* LXXXVIII [1915], 399–439). Some of the grammatical differences may be explained by the hypothesis that the Samaritan text preserves North Israelitic dialectal peculiarities, while the Masoretic text perpetuates a Judaean dialectal recension (so A. Sperber, *Hebrew Union College Annual,* XII-XIII [1937–38], 151 ff.). When the Septuagint diverges most from the Masoretic text, the Samaritan follows the latter with great fidelity (so H. M. Wiener, *The Expositor,* 8th Series, II [1911], 200–219, who criticizes Gesenius' methodology in his analysis of the Samaritan text).

Early in the Christian era the Samaritan Pentateuch was translated into the Aramaic dialect of the Samaritans. This version, called the Samaritan Targum, is a colloquial rendering which is distinguished from the Palestinian-Jewish Targums by lacking the literalism of the latter (E. Robertson, in *Saadya Studies,* pp. 166–176). The exegesis is popular and without influence from Jewish sources. See also E. ARAMAIC VERSIONS (TARGUMS), below.

There was also a Greek translation of the Samaritan Pentateuch (known as the Samaritikon), about fifty quotations of which are preserved in the notes on Origen's Hexapla. What its exact relationship to the Septuagint is has been debated, but the discovery of fragments of the version (Gen. 37; Deut. 24–29; ed. P. Glaue and A. Rahlfs, *Mitteilungen des Septuaginta-Unternehmens,* II, 1911) reveals that it was made from the Samaritan Pentateuch by translators familiar with the Septuagint.

Several Arabic translations of the Samaritan Pentateuch were made in the eleventh to the thirteenth century (P. Kahle, *Die arabischen Bibeluebersetzungen,* pp. x f.; and *The Cairo Geniza,* pp. 36–39).

BIBLIOGRAPHY: A. Rahlfs, *Fragmenta einer griechischen Uebersetzung des samaritanischen Pentateuchs,* 1911; A. von Gall, *Der hebraeische Pentateuch der Samaritaner,* 5 vols., 1914–18; Chaim Heller, *The Samaritan Pentateuch, an Adaptation of the Masoretic Text,* 1923; M. Gaster, *The Samaritans,* 1925; D. S. Sassoon, *Descriptive Catalogue of the . . . Samaritan MSS. in the Sassoon Library,* 1933; C. W. Dugmore, "Two Samaritan MSS in the Library of Queens College, Cambridge," *JTS,* XXXVI (1935), 131–147; Lea Goldberg, *Das samaritanische Pentateuchtargum,* 1935; E. Robertson, *Catalogue of the Samaritan Manuscripts in the John Rylands Library,* 1938.

E. ARAMAIC VERSIONS (TARGUMS): Five substantial fragments (dated *ca.* A.D. 700–900) of a Palestinian Pentateuch Targum, not Onkelos, were discovered in the famous Genizah of a synagogue in Old Cairo. The new Targum is often a free paraphrase with haggadic additions and occasionally presupposes an underlying Hebrew consonantal text differing from the Masoretic text. The language of the fragments is thought by Kahle to be first century Aramaic and, as such, to represent a much earlier stage in the history of the Targums than that of the other Targums. There is, however, no generally accepted dating of the various Targums.

According to Stenning, the Hebrew text presupposed by the Targum of Isaiah differs very slightly from the Masoretic text. In addition, the translation is generally faithful to the Hebrew; a notable exception, however, is the Targumist's bias when he "actually rewrites ch. 53, replacing it by one bearing no resemblance to the original" (P. Churgin, *Targum Jonathan*

[1927], p. 84). See also D. THE SAMARITAN PENTATEUCH.

BIBLIOGRAPHY: M. Neumark, *Lexikalische Untersuchungen zur Sprache der jerusalemischen Pentateuch-Targume*, 1905; A. Levy, *Das Targum zu Koheleth nach suedarabischen Handschriften*, 1905; Emil Brederek, *Konkordanz zum Targum Onkelos*, 1906; P. E. Kahle, *Masoreten des Westens*, Vols. I and II, 1927, 1930; Aapeli Saarisalo, "The Targum to the Book of Ruth," *Studia Orientalia* (Societas orientalis fennica), II (1928), 88–104; S. Silverstone, *Aquila and Onkelos*, 1931; A. Marmorstein, "Bemerkungen zu den neuentdeckten Fragmenten des jerusalemischen (palaestinensischen) Targums," *ZATW*, N. F. VIII (1931), 231–242; P. Churgin, "The Targum and the Septuagint," *AJSL*, L (1933), 41–65; A. Sperber, "The Targum Onkelos in its Relation to the Hebrew Masoretic Text," *Proceedings of the American Academy for Jewish Research*, VI (1934–35), 309–351; *idem*, "Peschitta und Onkelos," *Jewish Studies in Memory of G. A. Kohut* (1935), pp. 554-564; S. Wohl, *Das palaestinische Pentateuch-Targum*, 1935; V. Hamp, *Der Begriff "Wort" in den aramaeischen Bibeluebersetzungen*, 1938; C. J. Kosowski, *Otzar ha-Targum* (A Concordance to the Targum of Jonathan), 1940; Allen Wikgren, "The Targum and the New Testament," *JR*, XXIV (1944), 89–95; P. Churgin, *Targum Kethubim* (in Hebrew), 1945; J. F. Stenning, *The Targum of Isaiah*, 1949.

F. COPTIC VERSIONS: The largest collection of Coptic biblical manuscripts made available is the *Bibliothecae Pierpont Morgan codices coptici photographice expressi* . . . (1922, 56 vols. in 63). For a list of the contents of these volumes, as well as information regarding other biblical texts, see Winifred Kammerer, *A Coptic Bibliography* (1950). This latter now supplants A. Vaschalde, *Ce qui a été publié des versions coptes de la Bible* (1922) (originally published in *RB*, XXVIII-XXXI [1919–22]).

Gehman's study of Daniel reveals that the Sahidic version was translated from the Greek text of Theodotion with influence from Origen's Hexapla on a Hesychian background, and that the Bohairic version was made from the Hesychian form of the Hexaplaric Greek.

The Sahidic version of the Gospels reveals a complex character, combining elements found in the Alexandrian and Western families, and agreeing as well with certain of the readings of P^{45}. In the Acts the Sahidic shows a close affinity with the type of text in Codex Vaticanus (B). In the rest of the New Testament this version belongs to the Alexandrian recension.

In all parts of the New Testament the Bohairic version is freer from Western readings than is the Sahidic, and agrees closely with the Alexandrian recension.

The Qau papyrus codex of the Gospel of John in the sub-Achmimic dialect, dated by its editor in the third quarter of the fourth century, agrees most frequently with B, *aleph,* and L.

BIBLIOGRAPHY: Herbert Thompson, *The Coptic (Sahidic) Version of Certain Books of the Old Testament from a Papyrus in the British Museum*, 1908; Sir Herbert Thompson, *A Coptic Palimpsest Containing Joshua, Judges, Ruth, Judith and Esther in the Sahidic Dialect*, 1911; E. A. Wallis Budge, *Coptic Biblical Texts in the Dialects of Upper Egypt*, 1912; George Horner, *The Coptic Version of the New Testament in the Northern Dialect* . . . , 4 vols., 1898–1905; *idem, The Coptic Version of the New Testament in the Southern Dialect* . . . , 7 vols., 1911–24; Sir Herbert Thompson, *The Gospel of St. John According to the Earliest Coptic Manuscript*, 1924; W. H. Worrell, *The Coptic Manuscripts in the Freer Collection*, 1923; H. S. Gehman, "The Sahidic and Bohairic Versions of the Book of Daniel," *JBL*, XLVI (1927), 279–330; W. Till, *Die achmimische Version der Zwoelf Kleinen Profeten*, 1927; W. H. Worrell, *The Proverbs of Solomon in Sahidic*, 1931; F. H. Hallock, "The Coptic Old Testament," *AJSL*, XLIX (1932–33), 325–335; A. Boehlig, *Untersuchungen ueber die koptischen Proverbientexte*, 1936; Willem Grossow, *The Coptic Version of the Minor Prophets*, 1938; M. Malinine, "Fragment d'une version achmimique des Petits Prophètes," *Coptic Studies in Honour of W. E. Crum* (1950), pp. 365–416.

G. THE GOTHIC VERSION: In 1908 a vellum leaf from a bilingual Gothic-Latin codex was discovered at Antinöe in Egypt (Paul Glaue and Karl Helm, *ZNTW*, XI [1910], 1–38). Wilhelm Streitberg edited all the extant fragments of both Old Testament and New Testament and reconstructed the Greek *Vorlage* (*Die gotische Bibel*, 1908; 3rd ed., 1950). According to Michael Metlan, Streitberg's Greek text is in need of revision (*Journal of English and Germanic Philology*, XXXII [1933], 530–548). The University Library at Uppsala published a magnificent photographic facsimile of Codex Argenteus (*Codex argenteus Upsaliensis* . . . , 1927).

BIBLIOGRAPHY: P. J. Odefey, *Das gotische Lukas-Evangelium* (Diss. Kiel), 1908; Adolf Juelicher, "Die griechische Vorlage der gotischen Bibel," *ZDAL*, LII (1910), 365–387; Erich Mayr, *Die gotische Bibel, I: Matthaeus*, 1913, 2te Aufl., 1928; Hans Lietzmann, "Die Vorlage der gotischen Bibel," *ZDAL*, LVI (1919), 249–278; W. Limke, *Das gotische Markusevangelium*, 1920; G. W. S. Friedrichsen, *The Gothic Version of the Gospels, A Study of Its Style and Textual History*, 1926; *idem, The Gothic Version of the Epistles, A Study of Style and Textual History*, 1939; J. de Vries, *Wulfilae codices Ambrosiani rescripti epistularum evangelicarum textum Goticum exhibentes*, Florence, 1936; Fernand Mossé, "Bibliographia Gotica, A Bibliography of Writings on the Gothic Language, to the End of 1949," *Mediaeval Studies*, XII (1950), 237–324 (pp. 255–264 deal with the biblical version).

H. THE ARMENIAN VERSION: In general the Armenian version of the Old Testament is thought to follow carefully the Hexaplaric recension of the Septuagint. Gehman's research on Daniel reveals its affinities with an Origenian-Constantinopolitan type of text, with agreements also with the Hesychian witnesses and the Syriac.

It has been disputed whether the Armenian New Testament was translated from the Syriac (so J. A. Robinson, Conybeare, Merk, Blake, Baumstark) or directly from the Greek (so Macler, Lyonnet, and Colwell). As to type of New Testament text represented by the Armenian, Blake, Colwell, Lyonnet, and Williams find evidence of Caesarean traits.

Recently Lyonnet has investigated more thoroughly certain suggestions made by Baumstark, Peradze, and Essabalean that behind the present Armenian text of the Gospels there was an Armenian Diatessaron. As for the Apocalypse, Conybeare discerned five revisions.

BIBLIOGRAPHY: Artasches Abeghian, *Vorfragen zur Entstehungsgeschichte der altarmenischen Bibeluebersetzungen*, 1906; F. C. Conybeare, *The Armenian Version of Revelation*, 1907; Frédéric Macler, *Le texte arménien de l'évangile d'après Matthieu et Marc*, 1919; August Merk, "Die armenische Evangelien und ihre Vorlage," *Biblica*, VII (1926), 40–70; H. S. Gehman, "The Armenian Version of the Book of Daniel and its Affinities," *ZATW*, N.F. VII (1930), 82–99; E. C. Colwell, "The Caesarean Readings of Armenian Gospel Manuscripts," *Anglican Theological Review*, XVI (1934), 113–132; *idem*, "Slandered or Ignored: The Armenian Gospels," *Journal of Religion*, XVII (1937), 48–61; C. S. C. Williams, "Syriasms in the Armenian Text of the Gospels," *JTS*, XLIII (1942), 161–167; St. Lyonnet, *Les origines de la version arménienne et le Diatessaron*, 1950.

I. THE GEORGIAN VERSION: According to Blake the manuscript tradition of different parts of the Georgian Old Testament is not uniform. The original translations and later revisions were made at different times and from varying archetypes, namely, Armenian and Greek (Septuagint). The relation of the edition printed at Moscow in 1743 to the Armenian texts, in the Prophets at least, is much closer than has previously been supposed, being presumably a revision of a direct translation from the Armenian.

In the New Testament modern non-critical editions reproduce a Georgian text prepared in the tenth or eleventh century. The earliest known manuscripts of the Gospels are the Adysh manuscript (A.D. 897), Opiza manuscript (A.D. 913), and Tbet' (A.D. 995) which preserve two strains of Old Georgian text, both of which belong to the Caesarean family. A manuscript of Acts (A.D. 965, so Ropes, *The Text of Acts*, p. clxxxiii, n. 2), tested in four chapters, reveals many Western readings. The Book of Revelation, according to Lyonnet, appears to have been first translated into Georgian by St. Euthymius, the Athonite (*ca.* A.D. 978).

BIBLIOGRAPHY: F. C. Conybeare, "The Growth of the Peshitta Version of the New Testament illustrated from the Old Armenian and Georgian Versions," *AJT*, I (1897); *idem*, "The Old Georgian Version of Acts," *ZNTW*, XII (1911), 131–140; Franz Zorell, "Ursprung und Eigenart der georgischen Bibeluebersetzung," *Handes Amsorya*, XLI (1927), 669–680; R. P. Blake, *The Old Georgian Version of the Gospel of Mark, from the Adysh Gospels with the Variants of the Opiza and Tbet' Gospels* (=*Patrologia Orientalis*, XX, 3), 1929; . . . *of Matthew* (=*Patr. Orientalis*, XXIV, 1), 1933; . . . *of John* (with M. Brière) (=*Patr. Orientalis*, XXVI, 4), 1950; R. P. Blake, "Ancient Georgian Versions of the Old Testament," *HTR*, XIX (1926), 271–297; *idem*, "The Athos Codex of the Georgian Old Testament," *HTR*, XXII (1929), 33–56; *idem*, "Khanmeti Palimpsest Fragments of the Old Georgian Version of Jeremiah," *HTR*, XXV (1932), 225–272; cf. P. L. Hedley's corrections in *JTS*, XXXV (1933), 392–395; Stanislas Lyonnet in M. J. Lagrange, *Critique textuelle* (1935), 375–386, 460–463, 625; R. P. Blake and Sirarpie Der Nersessian, "The Gospels of Bert'ay; an Old Georgian Ms. of the Tenth Century," *Byzantion*, XVI (1942–43), 226–285; A. Shanidze, *Two Old Recensions of the Georgian Gospels according to Three Shatberd Manuscripts* (A.D. 897, 936, 973) (in Georgian), 1945; J. Molitor, "Die georgischen Bibeluebersetzung," *OC*, 4th Ser., I (1953), 23–29; *idem*, "Das Adysh-Tetraevangelium," *ibid.*, 30–55.

J. THE ETHIOPIC VERSION: It is estimated that outside Abyssinia there are today about 1,200 manuscripts of various parts of the Ethiopic Bible, most of them belonging to the sixteenth to eighteenth centuries. From a sampling of these it appears that the overwhelming majority present a form of text which was Arabicized in the fourteenth century. Very few manuscripts are older than this date. According to Gehman, in I Kings the Ethiopic text is based on a Greek text like that in B (Codex Vaticanus) with a strong Lucianic influence. There is no evidence, however, for a single unified text of the Ethiopic Bible, influenced throughout by the same Greek source. To the contrary, Gleave's research supports Charles' view (based on Malachi and Lamentations) that the Ethiopic is indebted to Symmachus and other portions of the Hexapla.

In the New Testament the original translators at times followed the Greek text slavishly, and at other times, perhaps where the Greek proved too difficult for them, they paraphrased wildly (so Montgomery). An analysis of sporadic quotations of the Synoptic Gospels in several Ethiopic ecclesiastical writers seems to reveal kinship with the Old Syriac text (so Vööbus).

BIBLIOGRAPHY: August Heider, *Die aethiopische Bibeluebersetzung* . . . , I: *Bibelkritische Abhandlung*, 1902; F. M. E. Pereira, *Job* (*Patrologia Orientalis*, II, 5), 1905; *Esther* (*P.O.*, IX, 1), 1911; *Esdras et Néhémie* (*P.O.*, XIII, 5), 1919; J. Oscar Boyd, *The Octateuch in Ethiopic*, I and II (Gen., Ex., and Lev.), 1909–1911; F. M. E. Pereira, "O livro do profeta Amós e a sua versão etiopica," *Academia das sciencias de Lisboa; Boletim da segunda classe*, XI (1918), 472–534; Francesco da Bassano edited the Ethiopic Bible at Asmara, 5 vols., 1911–21, 2nd ed. of New Testament, 1934; Oscar Loefgren, *Die aethiopische Uebersetzung des Propheten Daniel*, 1927; *idem*, *Jona, Nahum, Habakuk, Zephanja, Haggai, Sacharja und Maleachi aethiopisch*, 1930; S. A. B. Mercer, *The Ethiopic Text of the Book of Ecclesiastes*, 1931; H. S. Gehman, "The Old Ethiopic Version of I Kings and Its Affinities," *JBL*, L (1931), 81–114; James A. Montgomery, "The Ethiopic Text of Acts of the Apostles," *HTR*, XXVII (1934), 169–205; H. C. Gleave, *The Ethiopic Version of the Song of Songs Critically Edited*, 1951; Arthur Vööbus, *Die Spuren eines aelteren aethiopischen Evangelientextes im Lichte der literarischen Monumente*, 1951. For excellent annotated bibliographies see George F. Black, "Ethiopica and Amharica," *Bulletin of the New York Public Library*, XXXII (1928), 443–481, 528–562; C. Conti Rossini in *Aevum*, I (1927), 459–624 (covers 1915–27); *Aevum*, X (1936), 467–587 (covers 1927–36); *Rassegna di studi etiopici*, IV (1944–45), 1–132 (covers 1936–45); J. Simon in *Orientalia*, XXI (1952), 47–66 (covers 1946–51). See also Silvio Zanutto, *Bibliografia etiopica*, II: *Manoscritti etiopici*, 1932; K. J. Luethi in *Gutenbergmuseum*, XXII, 5–38, reprinted with additions in his *Aethiopisch in der Schweiz*, 1936.

K. THE NUBIAN VERSION: During the sixth century the northern kingdom of Nubia (the land between Egypt and Abyssinia) received Christianity from Monophysite missionaries. Portions of an Old Nubian lectionary for Christmastide survive, dating from the tenth or eleventh century and containing for each day pericopes from the Apostolos and the Gospel (namely, short sections from Romans, Galatians, Philippians, Hebrews, Matthew, and Luke).

BIBLIOGRAPHY: For the history of Nubian Christianity, see G. Roeder, *ZKG*, XXXIII (1912), 364–398; and Ugo Monneret de Villard, *Storia della Nubia cristiana*, 1938. The fragments were edited first by H. Schaefer and K. Schmidt in *SBA*, phil.-hist. kl. (Nov. 8, 1906), 774–785; and definitively re-edited by F. L. Griffith, *Abhandlungen der koeniglich Preussischen Akademie der Wissenschaften*, phil.-hist. Kl. (1913), no. 8.

L. THE SOGDIAN VERSION: The Sogdian language, the easternmost member of the Indo-European family of languages, flourished in Central Asia during the second half of the first millennium of the Christian era. Portions of Matthew, Luke, and John in the form of a lectionary, as well as small fragments of I Corinthians and Galatians, have been discovered in this Iranian dialect. According to a study by Peters, the Gospel material was translated from a Syriac base substantially identical with the Peshitta, but containing several noteworthy variations.

Portions of Psalms 94–99, 118 (119), and 121–136 (122–137) have been discovered in Pahlavi, an Iranian language related to Sogdian, dating from about the seventh century (edited by F. C. Andreas and Kaj Barr in *SBA*, 1933, 91–152).

BIBLIOGRAPHY: F. W. K. Mueller, "Neutestamentliche Bruchstuecke in soghdischer Sprache," *SBA* (1907), 260–270; *idem, Abhandlungen der koeniglich Preussischen Akademie der Wissenschaften*, phil.-hist. Kl. (1912), no. 2; J. R. Harris, *Side-Lights on N. T. Research* (1908), pp. 116–124; Curt Peters, *OC*, 3te Serie, XI (1936), 153–162.

M. THE OLD SLAVIC VERSION: On the basis of an examination of 500 readings in the Old Slavic Psalter, Josef Vajs found that 449 preserve a Lucianic (Greek) type of text, and that the others were influenced by the Latin Vulgate (*Byzantinoslavica,* VIII [1939–46], 55–86).

It appears certain that the Old Slavic Gospels existed first in lectionary form, having been translated from a Greek Gospel lectionary. Later additions were made in order to embrace the full text of the Gospels. According to analyses made by Vajs, the textual type of the Gospels is fundamentally Byzantine in which are embedded many Palestinian and Caesarean readings. (The work of Schweigl, who found strong Alexandrian influence, *Biblica,* XXIV [1943], 289–303, is vitiated by an imperfect acquaintance with textual methodology). The Apostolos, according to Jagić, presents a text substantially like that of the Greek *textus receptus.* The Apocalypse stands apart from the rest of the version, not having been translated until the twelfth century (so Oblak).

Whether influence from the Latin Vulgate can be detected in the Old Slavic has been debated, Pogorělov (*Sborník fil. fak. Univ. Komenského, Bratislavě,* III, 32 [1925], 207–216) arguing for such influence; Meillet (*Revue des études slaves,* VI [1926], 39–41), against it. See also **II. Modern Versions: W. SLAVIC VERSIONS.**

BIBLIOGRAPHY: V. Oblak, "Die kirchenslavische Uebersetzung der Apokalypse," *Archiv fuer slavische Philologie,* XIII (1891), 321–361; V. Jagić, "Zum altkirchenslavischen Apostolus," in *Sitzungsberichte d. Ak. d. Wiss. in Wien,* phil.-hist. Kl., 191, 2 (1919); Andrej Snoj, "Veteroslavicae versionis evangeliorum . . . momentum," *Biblica,* III (1922), 180–187; Josef Vajs, *Evangelium sv. Matouše. Text rekonstruovaný,* 1935; . . . *Marka,* 1935; . . . *Lukáše,* 1936; . . . *Jana,* 1936; R. P. Casey and Silva Lake, "A New Edition of the Old Slavic Gospels," *JBL,* LV (1936), 195–209; J. Hamm, "Ueber den gotischen Einfluss auf die altkirchenslavische Bibeluebersetzung," *Zeitschrift fuer vergleichende Sprachwissenschaft,* LXVII (1942), 112–128; J. Bonfante and B. M. Metzger, "The Old Slavic Version of the Gospel according to Luke," *JBL,* LXXIII (1954), 217–236 (with a survey of previous investigations).

N. THE ARABIC VERSIONS: In opposition to the prevailing opinion, several scholars have argued in favor of a pre-Islamic date for the earliest Arabic versions (e.g., Anton Baumstark, *Islamica,* IV [1931], 562–575; *OC,* 3te Serie, IX [1934], 165–188, and 278–279; and Curt Peters, *Acta orientalia,* XVIII [1940], 124–137; *Revista degli studi orientali,* XX [1942], 129–143).

As regards the Pentateuch, Rhode found that two Christian Arabic versions were current in Egypt: a version from the Bohairic used by the Jacobites and one from the Sahidic used by the Melchites; both were influenced by the Hebrew and Samaritan texts.

According to Vaccari (*Biblica,* II [1921], 401–423; III [1922], 401–423; cf. IV [1923], 312–314) the Arabic text of the prophetic books in the Paris Polyglot was translated at Alexandria by the priest El-Alam (ninth or tenth century) from a Greek text close to Codex Alexandrinus. Gehman's study of the Arabic version of the Book of Daniel in the Paris and London Polyglot Bibles shows that it was rendered from a Greek Hexaplaric text of Constantinople in a recension superior to Codex Alexandrinus and all other witnesses.

In the New Testament Peters, who tested sample passages from all four Gospels in a group which Guidi found to be translated from Greek, discovered not a few Tatianisms (*OC,* 3te Serie, XI [1936], 188–211). Levin's analysis of Matthew and Mark in two Arabic manuscripts translated from Greek discloses that in addition to Tatianisms many readings characteristic of the Caesarean text are also present. See also **D. THE SAMARITAN PENTATEUCH.**

BIBLIOGRAPHY: P. E. Kahle, *Die arabische Bibeluebersetzungen,* 1904; H. Spiegel, *Saadia al-Fajjûmî's arabische Danielversion,* 1906; J. C. Hughes, *De Lagarde's Ausgabe der arabischen Uebersetzung des Pentateuchs,* 1920; J. F. Rhode, *The Arabic Versions of the Pentateuch in the Church of Egypt,* 1921; H. S. Gehman, "The 'Polyglot' Arabic Text of Daniel and its Affinities," *JBL,* XLIV (1925), 327–352; P. E. Algermissen, *Die Pentateuchzitate Ibn Ḥazm,* 1933; O. Löfgren, *Studien zu den arabischen Danieluebersetzungen mit besonderer Beruecksichtigung der christlichen Texte,* 1936; Bernard Levin, *Die griechisch-arabische Evangelien-Uebersetzung . . . ,* 1938; George Graf, *Geschichte der christlichen arabischen Literatur,* I (1944), 85–195; P. E. Kahle, *The Cairo Geniza,* 1947.

O. THE ANGLO-SAXON VERSION: Investigation of the type of Latin text underlying the Anglo-Saxon version reveals that it was a mixture of various recensions of the Vulgate (with Alcuin's and the Irish recensions prominent) along with continuing strains of Old Latin texts. It may even be (so Peters) that the Anglo-Saxon preserves a Tatianic element, transmitted via the Old Latin. In any case, the view advocated by Drake, L. M. Harris, and Bright, that the type of text in Matthew differs from that in Mark and Luke, and both from that in John, is based on an incomplete examination of the data; Glunz's thorough analyses reveal no marked differences of type of text among the four Gospels.

BIBLIOGRAPHY: Allison Drake, *The Authorship of the West Saxon Gospels,* 1894; Robert Handke, *Ueber das Verhaeltnis der westsaechsischen Evangelien-Uebersetzung zum lateinischen Original,* 1896; L. M. Harris, *Studies in the Anglo-Saxon Version of the Gospels,* Part I: *The Form of the Latin Original . . . ,* 1901; James W. Bright, *The Gospel of Saint John [Matthew, Mark, Luke] in West-Saxon . . . ,* 1904–6; S. J. Crawford (ed.), *The Old English Version of the Heptateuch . . . ,* 1922, Hans Glunz, *Die lateinische Vorlage der westsaechsischen Evangelien-Version,* 1928; G. P. Krapp, *The Junius Manuscript* [of Caedmon's paraphrases], 1931; *idem, The Paris Psalter and the Meters of Boethius,* 1932; Curt Peters, "Der Diatessaron-text von Mt. 2, 9 und die westsaechsische Evangelien-version," *Biblica,* XXIII (1942), 323–332.

II. Modern Versions:

A. AFRIKAANS VERSION. See **E. DUTCH VERSIONS.**

B. BOHEMIAN (CZECH) VERSIONS, and **BULGARIAN VERSIONS.** See **W. SLAVIC VERSIONS.**

C. CELTIC VERSIONS: In 1932 the Reverend Ernest E. Joynt of the Irish Methodist Church published at Dublin his revision of Mark in present-day Irish. Other portions of the New Testament followed, and the entire New Testament appeared in 1951. The final revision of the manuscript of Joynt (who died shortly before the work was completed) was undertaken by the Reverend C. W. Quin. In the opinion of Douglas Hyde, expressed in a letter to the Hiberian Bible Society, Joynt's version is superior to previous ones, and "gives the sense of the Greek without any circumlocution whatever and still in a language quite intelligible."

BIBLIOGRAPHY: Hibernian Bible Society, *Report* (1933), p. 8; R. W. Jackson, *The Bible in Ireland* (1950), pp. 18–19.

D. DANISH VERSIONS. See **V. SCANDINAVIAN VERSIONS.**

E. DUTCH VERSIONS: H. C. Voorhoeve and N. A. J. Voorhoeve prepared for the use of Plymouth Brethren in The Netherlands their translation of the New Testament (1877). This was based on the Greek text underlying J. N. Darby's version. A third edition appeared in 1931. A second edition of Kuenen and Oort's version of the New Testament was published in 1915. A. M. Brouwer and H. Th. Obbink, of the University of Utrecht, published three large volumes of selections of their translation of the Bible (Amsterdam, 1917–27).

A good translation by Roman Catholic scholars (R. Jansen, B. Alfrink, J. Cools, *et al.*) was published in honor of Petrus Canisius in five volumes (Amsterdam, 1936–39). Another Roman Catholic translation, *De katholieke Bijbel,* less satisfactory than the "Canisius" edition, was prepared by two Franciscan scholars, Laetus Himmelreich and Crispinus Smits, who translated the Old Testament and the New Testament respectively (Bruegge, 1938).

In 1928 an interdenominational committee with F. W. Grosheide as chairman, which had been at work since 1911, was sponsored by the Netherlands Bible Society and commissioned to produce a version in accord with modern Dutch idiom and based upon the oldest attainable text. The New Testament was published at Amsterdam in 1939; the Bible in 1951.

Afrikaans, which is a Dutch dialect that was reduced to written form about 1872, became the medium of a version of Genesis (Paarl, 1893), translated by S. J. Du Toit and others. A committee, including D. G. Du Toit, J. D. Kestall, and B. B. Keet, prepared a translation of the Bible which the British and Foreign Bible Society published at Capetown in 1943. Before the Bible had actually been issued 30,000 copies had been ordered and paid for; 300,000 copies were sold within the first two years of its publication.

BIBLIOGRAPHY: C. C. De Bruin, *De Statenbijbel en zijn voorgangers,* 1937.

F. ENGLISH VERSIONS: 1. PROTESTANT (AND OTHER) TRANSLATIONS:

A group of about twenty scholars, whose identity was not disclosed beyond the fact that they represented various sections of the Christian Church, prepared *The Twentieth Century New Testament,* translating Westcott and Hort's Greek text. This was published at London in three parts between 1898 and 1901, and a revision in 1904. Within general subdivisions the books were arranged in what was regarded as their probable chronological order (thus, Mark precedes Matthew).

James Moffatt's *Historical New Testament* (Edinburgh, 1901) is a new translation, in traditional "biblical" English, of the books of the New Testament "arranged in the order of their literary growth and according to the dates of the documents" (as determined by the critical hypotheses prevalent at the beginning of the century).

A. S. Way, the noted translator of Homer, Vergil, and other classics, published his rendering of *The Letters of St. Paul to Seven Churches and Three Friends* (London, 1901). The second edition (1903) contained also the *Letter to the Hebrews.* The translation is marked by a judicious use of expansion, particularly of transitional connectives.

In 1903 Richard F. Weymouth, formerly head master of the Mill Hill School, produced *The New Testament in Modern Speech,* edited and partly revised by E. Hampden-Cook. It is a dignified and idiomatic translation into everyday English which seeks to render with great exactness the tenses of the Greek verb. (See Weymouth's pamphlet, *On the Rendering into English of the Greek Aorist and Perfect Tenses . . . ,* 1894). The underlying Greek text is Weymouth's Resultant Greek Testament, based on the best critical scholarship of the time. The first American edition, newly revised by J. A. Robertson, was published at Boston in 1943.

The Corrected English New Testament, A Revision of the "Authorized" Version (by Nestle's Resultant Text) was prepared by Samuel Lloyd (New York, 1905).

In 1912 the American Baptist Publication Society issued an "Improved Edition" of the Bible Union Version of 1864. Where the word "baptize" occurs it is followed by the word "immerse" enclosed in parentheses. In several passages the translation anticipated the rendering of the Revised Standard Version (1952), as, e.g., the translation of *'almah* in Isa. 7:14 as "young woman." Instead of italics, brackets are used to indicate words not in the original but supplied because of the requirements of English idiom.

James Moffatt's second translation (Edinburgh, 1913) was based upon von Soden's edition of the Greek New Testament, with several transpositions of verses, paragraphs, and chapters. In 1924 he published a translation of the Old Testament. Following the practice of several French translations and Matthew Arnold, Moffatt rendered the divine name ("Lord," "Jehovah") by "the Eternal." Both Testaments are characterized by a certain freshness of phraseology and sentence structure. In 1935 a "revised and final edition" of the Moffatt Bible was published.

The New Testament, An American Translation, utilizing the common language of everyday life, was prepared by Edgar J. Goodspeed (Chicago, 1923), based on the Westcott and Hort Greek text. *The Old Testament, An American Translation* appeared in 1927, prepared by T. J. Meek (University of Toronto), Leroy Waterman (University of Michigan), A. R. Gordon (University of Montreal), and J. M. P. Smith (University of Chicago), who was responsible also for the general editorial oversight. This edition contains an appendix of 91 pages listing emendations of the Hebrew which the translators preferred to the Masoretic text. In 1931 Goodspeed's New Testament was published with the Old Testament translation as *The Bible, An American Translation.* In 1939 there appeared *The Complete Bible, An American Translation,* consisting of T. J. Meek's stylistic revision of the Old Testament, Goodspeed's new translation of the Apocryphal books, and Goodspeed's New Testament.

The Riverside New Testament was translated by William G. Ballantine from Nestle's Greek text (1923; revised ed., 1934). It is an eclectic rendering with acknowledged dependence upon several previous translations.

G. C. Martin and T. H. Robinson edited ten pamphlets of *Books of the Old Testament in Colloquial Speech,* translated by various scholars and published by the National Adult School Union (London, 1923 ff.).

To mark the first hundred years of service of the American Baptist Publication Society, Mrs. Helen B. Montgomery, of Rochester, N. Y., published *The Centenary Translation of the New Testament* (2 vols., Philadelphia, 1924). She supplied her modern speech translation with colloquial subject headings, e.g., "A 'Close-up' of Sin," "Paul's Swan Song," and "Orchestrate Your Virtues."

A professor of Greek at Union University (Tennessee), Charles B. Williams, published *The New Testament, A Translation in the Language of the People* (Boston, 1937; reprinted, Chicago, 1950), based on Westcott and Hort's Greek text. Williams paid strict attention to the exact shades of meaning of the Greek tenses, especially with regard to the verbal "aspects" (*Aktionsarten*), but in so doing he occasionally overtranslated the Greek.

The Berkeley Version of the New Testament (Berkeley, California, 1945) is the work of Gerrit Verkuyl, who for many years was on the Board of Christian Education of the Presbyterian Church, U.S.A. Using chiefly Tischendorf's eighth edition of the Greek text (1869–72), Verkuyl's aim was to produce "a translation less interpretative than Moffatt's, more cultured in language than Goodspeed's, more American than Weymouth's, and freer from the King James Version than the Revised Standard [proved to be]" (Verkuyl, in *The Bible Translator,* Vol. II, No. 2 [April, 1951], 81).

The New Testament in Basic English (Cambridge, 1941) is a translation prepared by a committee under the direction of S. H. Hooke, Professor of Old Testament in the University of London. Basic English, which has a vocabulary of 850 words, was in this case supplemented by the addition of 50 special biblical words and 100 other words listed as giving most help in the reading of English verse. *The Old Testament in Basic English* was completed in the year 1950.

The New Testament Letters, prefaced and paraphrased by J. W. C. Wand, Bishop of London (Oxford, 1946), is a dignified rendering which expands the more difficult passages.

The New World Translation of the Christian Greek Scriptures is a more or less faithful rendering of Westcott and Hort's Greek text into vernacular English, published by the Watchtower Bible and Tract Society for the use of Jehovah's Witnesses (Brooklyn, 1950). The footnotes contain a certain amount of technical information regarding variant readings in manuscripts and early versions, but this is mingled with totally irrelevant information from various translations into Hebrew, made in the sixteenth and succeeding centuries. These latter are thought to give authority for the introduction of "Jehovah" into 237 passages in the New Testament. One of the characteristics of the version is an attempt to render each major Greek word always by the same English equivalent, irrespective of the requirements of the context. (For a critique of its Unitarianism, see B. M. Metzger, *TT,* X [1952], 65–85). The first of three projected volumes of the Witnesses' rendering of the Old Testament was issued in 1953. Among other characteristics, it follows Robert Young's idiosyncrasy in deliberately ignoring the force of the waw consecutive.

The Revised Standard Version of the New Testament, published in February, 1946, is a revision (authorized by churches through their educational boards associated in the International Council of Religious Education) of the American Standard Version (1901). It was prepared by a committee of translators from more than twenty theological seminaries and universities, with Luther A. Weigle as chairman. The work of revision was begun in 1930, suspended in 1932 because of lack of financial support, and resumed in 1937. The aim of the committee was to produce a version which retained more of the literary beauty of the King James Version than did the Revision of 1901, and at the same time to make such alterations as were deemed necessary in the light of increased knowledge of the text, vocabulary, and grammar of the Scriptures. The Old Testament was published in September, 1952. This differs from the 1901 revision in returning to the King James' use of "Lord" (instead of "Jehovah") and in a somewhat greater reliance upon variant readings supported by ancient versions, as against the Masoretic Hebrew text. A revision of the Apocryphal books is in progress. (See two pamphlets of essays issued by members of the Revision Committee, *An Introduction to the Revised Standard Version of the New Testament,* 1946; and *An Introduction to . . . the Old Testament,* 1952.)

J. B. Phillips, an Anglican priest, prepared a rendering of the New Testament Epistles (*Letters to Young Churches,* New York, 1948), characterized by frequent expansion and paraphrase couched in flowing vernacular English. It is based on Souter's edition of the Greek text which inferentially lies behind the 1881 English Revision. Phillips also published *The Gospels Translated into Modern English* (New York, 1953).

E. V. Rieu, translator of several Greek and Latin classics and editor of the Penguin Classics since 1945, published his rendering of the Gospels in the Penguin series (1952); this had been preceded by his privately printed rendering of Mark (1951). The translation is characterized by dignified simplicity.

In 1937 the Society for the Promotion of Christian Knowledge asked Charles Kingsley Williams to prepare a translation of the New Testament in simplified English (involving the vocabulary of about 2000 common words listed by a group of educators in the *Interim Report on Vocabulary Selection,* 1936). Williams entitled his rendering of Souter's Greek text, *The New Testament, A New Translation in Plain English* (London, 1952).

2. ROMAN CATHOLIC TRANSLATIONS: With Cuthbert Lattey, S.J., as the general editor, there began to appear in 1913, *The Westminster Version of the Sacred Scriptures,* based on the original Hebrew and Greek. The New Testament was finished in 1935, and several books of the Old Testament have been published.

Shortly before his death in 1913 Francis A. Spencer, O.P., completed a rather free translation of the Greek New Testament; this was edited and published by C. J. Callan and J. A. McHugh (New York, 1937). Vulgate readings when different from the Greek are given in brackets or in footnotes.

A revision of the Challoner-Rheims version, resting upon the Latin Vulgate, was published by a group of twenty-seven Roman Catholic scholars under the patronage of the Episcopal Committee of the Confraternity of Christian Doctrine (Paterson, N. J., 1941). Where the Latin and the Greek differ, a rendering of the latter is given in footnotes. Under the patronage of the same Episcopal Committee a group of members of the Catholic Biblical Association of America is at work translating the Old Testament from the Hebrew. The Book of Genesis was published in 1948; the Psalms and Canticles in 1950; and the books from Genesis to Ruth, 1952. A curious typographical error appears in the first printing of the last-named volume. In Lev. 11:30, among the list of lizard-like animals forbidden as food, there is listed the "skunk," a misprint for "skink."

Monsignor Ronald A. Knox's rendering of the Vulgate New Testament (London, 1944) and of the Old Testament including Apocrypha (two volumes, 1949), is a fresh, sagacious, and skillful piece of work. (See Matthew P. Stapleton, "Catholic Bible Translations," *JBR,* XIV [1946], 198-202).

3. JEWISH TRANSLATIONS: Claude G. Montefiore, a liberal Jewish scholar, published in two volumes in 1896 and 1899 nearly the whole of the Old Testament in his *Bible for Home Reading.* He also included a version of the Synoptic Gospels in his two-volume commentary on *The Synoptic Gospels* (1911; 2nd ed., 1927).

In 1917 the Jewish Publication Society of America issued *The Holy Scriptures According to the Masoretic Text, A New Translation,* which was prepared by a committee of Jewish scholars with Max L. Margolis as editor-in-chief. It aims to combine the spirit of Jewish tradition with the results of biblical scholarship. (See M. L. Margolis, *The Story of Bible Translations,* 1917; and Alexander Sperber, "A New Bible Translation," *Alexander Marx Jubilee Volume,* Eng. Section [1950], pp. 547-580.)

See also BIBLES, ANNOTATED.

BIBLIOGRAPHY: J. G. Carleton, *The Part of Rheims in the Making of the English Bible,* 1902; M. W. Jacobus, *Roman Catholic and Protestant Bibles Compared,* 1905; Henry Barker, *English Bible Versions,* 1907; A. W. Pollard, *Records of the English Bible,* 1911; Joseph H. Penniman, *A Book About the English Bible,* 1919; Laura H. Wild, *The Romance of the English Bible,* 1929; P. Marion Simms, *The Bible in America, Versions that have Played Their Part in the Making of the Republic,* 1936; H. W. Robinson (ed.), *The Bible in Its Ancient and English Versions,* 1940; C. C. Butterworth, *The Literary Lineage of the King James Bible,* 1941; David Daiches, *The King James Version of the English Bible,* 1941; Harold R. Willoughby, *Soldiers' Bibles through the Centuries,* 1944; Ira M. Price, *The Ancestry of Our English Bible,* 2nd rev. ed., by W. A. Irwin and A. P. Wikgren, 1949, corrected ed., 1951; Luther A. Weigle, *The English New Testament from Tyndale to the Revised Standard Version,* 1949; A. P. Wikgren, "The Use of Marginal Notes in the English Bible," *Crozer Quarterly,* XXVII (1950), 143-153; Stanley Rypens, *The Book of Thirty Centuries,* 1951; Herbert Gordon May, *Our English Bible in the Making,* 1952; Hugh Pope, *English*

Versions of the Bible, revised and amplified by S. Bullough, 1952.

G. FINNISH VERSIONS: In 1891 Ludvig Enkvist published at Porvoossa his translation of St. John's Gospel. This was the first portion of Scripture to appear in roman type. Since about 1910 Scripture editions have generally been in roman character, except those in the Karelian dialect. These latter, which were published by the Russian Orthodox Missionary Society, use the Cyrillic characters. In the twentieth century a scholarly revision of the Finnish Bible, on the basis of the oldest accessible texts of the original languages, was prepared by a group of professors. The New Testament was finished in 1913 and was tentatively approved by the Lutheran Church Assembly. Tentative editions of various parts of the Old Testament were issued up to 1930. As few criticisms were received, the whole was re-examined by the committee in 1931 and a final text prepared. In 1933 the Lutheran Church Assembly tentatively approved the Old Testament, and both Testaments were approved fully in 1938. They were published by the Finnish Bible Society at Helsinki in 1939.

BIBLIOGRAPHY: Arthur Hjelt, "Mikael Agricola, der erste finnische Bibeluebersetzer," *Theologische Studien, Theodor Zahn . . . dargebracht* (1908), pp. 91-106; O. M. Norlie (ed.), *The Translated Bible* (1934), pp. 158-166; A. F. Puukko "Die Lutherbibel und die finnische Bibeluebersetzung," *Zeitschrift fuer systematische Theologie,* XVIII (1941), 68-75; *idem,* "Mikael Agricola som finsk Bibelöversättare," *Festskrift tillägnad hovpredikanten Isaac Béen . . .* (1948), pp. 13-28.

H. FRENCH VERSIONS: Among Protestant translations are the following. Pastor A. Decoppet published (Paris, 1903) a rendering of Westcott and Hort's edition of the Greek New Testament, which is less modern in style than Stapfer's translation (1889). A revision of the Ostervald text, prepared under the direction of the Synod of the Reformed Churches and published by the Bible Society of France, appeared in 1910. This has been revised several times. Maurice Goguel, Henri Monnier, and several other scholars published their modern vernacular version of the New Testament in 1929. It contains notes regarding variant readings in manuscripts and ancient versions. The Bible du Centenaire de la Jeunesse, based on the latest results of modern scholarship and published by the Protestant Bible Society of Paris, appeared in 1947.

Among Roman Catholic translations are the following: M.-J. Lagrange of the École Biblique at Jerusalem, published translations of the Gospels in his commentaries (1921-29). In 1932 the Pieuse Société Saint Paul issued a version of the Bible based upon the Vulgate. The Belgian scholar, Bernard Botte, O.S.B., published a translation of the Greek text of the New Testament, with notes that deal with textual and exegetical difficulties (Turnhout, 1944).

A translation which may supplant the widely-used version by Abbé Crampon (1905) is being issued in several small volumes under the direction of the École Biblique of Jerusalem (the Gospels were published at Paris in 1948). The rendering, which is not so literalistic as Crampon's, was made from the original languages and is accompanied by two series of notes, one justifying the variant readings adopted, and the other explaining difficult passages. Paul George Passelecq, a Benedictine at Maredsous who, while in a concentration camp during World War II, formed the resolve to bring the Bible to Roman Catholics in the vernacular, published his translation of the Gospels (Brussels, 1946), the New Testament (1948) and the Bible (1950). The rendering follows somewhat Segond's (Protestant) version, but is simpler and more colloquial.

BIBLIOGRAPHY: D. Lortsch, *Histoire de la Bible en France . . . ,* 1910.

I. GERMAN VERSIONS: A translation of the Bible by F. E. Schlachter was published at Biel, Switzerland, in 1903-4. In 1920 Ludwig Albrecht, a Free Church pastor at Bremen, finished his rendering of the New Testament (6th ed., 1938). The translation, which is free, clear, and idiomatic, has been used widely in Bible classes for the laity and in schools for advanced pupils.

The "Menge Bible" is generally recognized as one of the very best German versions of the Bible. Hermann Menge worked tirelessly for twenty years on his translation, finishing it on his eighty-fifth birthday. It was published by the Privilegierte Wuerttembergische Bibelanstalt of Stuttgart in 1926. Like Luther, however, Menge continued to improve his work, and, a few months before his death on January 8, 1939, in his ninety-seventh year, he gave to the Bibelanstalt his final revision, which was incorporated in the eleventh edition and represents the "textus receptus" of the Menge Bible.

Theodor Daechsel, a Silesian pastor, published in 1928 a rendering of von Soden's Greek text under the following title, *Die Schriften des Neuen Testaments nach ihrem urspruenglichen Wortsinn in die deutsche Sprache der Gegenwart wort- und sinngetreu uebertragen.* Despite the aim expressed in the title, Daechsel's work is marred occasionally by anachronisms, fanciful opinions, and poor German.

After twenty-five years of work a committee, appointed by the Synod of Churches of the Canton of Zurich, issued a revision of the Old Zwingli version, on the four hundredth anniversary of the death of Zwingli (Zurich, 1931). It is considered by many to be one of the best modern German translations, particularly for the Old Testament.

In 1931 Adolf Schlatter published at Stuttgart his translation of Nestle's Greek text, accompanied by a few notes.

Under the Nazis, Wilhelm Teudt made a revision designed to remove "Jewish taints." The Psalms, thus Germanized, were published at Leipzig in 1934. The Gospel of John was made more palatable to anti-Semites by omitting or altering Hebrew words and Old Testament references (Leipzig, 1936). In 1934–35 Wilhelm Michaelis published in *Kroeners Taschenausgabe,* Band 120/121 (Leipzig), his translation of the New Testament. This provides in parentheses alternative translations of words and phrases.

A revision of Luther's version of the New Testament and Psalms, prepared by a committee appointed by the German Bible Societies and by the German Evangelical Church, was published (Stuttgart, 1938) as a *Probe-Ausgabe* ("test edition"). The aim of the committee was to give the church a reliable version, based on Nestle's Greek text, presenting Luther's understanding of the Bible and keeping as far as possible the unique treasure of Luther's language. The Old Testament was also issued as a *Probe-Ausgabe* (Stuttgart, 1951). After the Bible has been in circulation for several years, a committee will give consideration to criticisms by those who have used the version, and a revised form will then be submitted to the Landeskirche (regional Evangelical Churches) for official approval.

In 1939 a so-called Concordant version of the New Testament was published at Stepenitz, prepared under the direction of A. E. Knoch. In this version each Greek word is always translated by the same German equivalent. Friedrich Pfaefflin issued a rendering of the New Testament in modern vernacular German (Heilbronn, 1938; 2nd ed., 1949).

In 1946 Ludwig Thimme, a Lutheran pastor, published at Stuttgart a translation of the New Testament in beautiful, fluent German.

Among Roman Catholic translations are the following: Jakob Ecker, professor at Priesterseminar, Trier, published a translation of the New Testament based on the Vulgate text (Trier, 1915). Peter Ketter's rendering of the New Testament was made at the request of the then Bishop of Rottenburg, Paul Wilhelm von Keppler (Stuttgart, 1915). It was revised in 1937 on the basis of Merk's Greek text; a third edition appeared in 1948. Fritz Tillmann translated Vogels' Greek text (Muenchen, 1927; 7th ed., 1947). J. E. Niederhuber, Hochschulprofessor at Regensburg, published a translation of the Greek New Testament in 1931. Two members of the Order of Capuchian Monks, Konstantin Roesch and Eugen Henne, published a translation, the former rendering the New Testament (Paderborn, 1932), the latter the Old Testament (1936).

In 1944 Johann Perk published at Koeln a translation of the New Testament which in some respects resembles that of Roesch, but in general is more literalistic. The series, *Das Neue Testament uebersetzt und kurz erklaert,* is an original and scholarly translation from the Greek by Josef Schmid, Alfred Wikenhauser, and others; the concluding volume (ninth, containing Revelation) appeared in 1947. P. Riessler and R. Storr translated respectively the Old and the New Testaments (Mainz, 1949). J. F. Allioli and K. Thieme rendered the New Testament from the Vulgate, making comparison with the Greek (Feiburg/B, 1949); this is called "Herders Laienbibel." In 1950 O. Karrer translated and annotated the New Testament (Muenchen). Seeking since 1919 to put inexpensive portions of the Scripture in the vernacular into the hands of the laity, Pius Parsch, a monk at Klosterneuberg, Austria, finished his rendering of the entire Bible in 1952 (see *TT,* X [1953], 45 ff.).

A special group of German versions are those printed in Hebrew characters. It was Moses Mendelssohn, whom the *Jewish Encyclopedia* calls "the 'Third Moses,' with whom begins a new era in Judaism," who produced a German translation of the Pentateuch, printed in Hebrew characters, which came to be warmly admired by German-speaking Jews (Berlin, 1780–83). He translated the Psalter in 1783; the Song of Solomon in 1789. Luther's version of the New Testament was transliterated into rabbinic characters by Judah D'Allemand (London, 1820). Mendelssohn's work was continued by Salomon Kasselberg, who published the Old Testament at Basel in 1825. A translation by H. Arnheim and M. Sachs aided by J. Fuerst and L. Zunz (all under the editorship of Zunz), was published in Berlin in 1937. See also **Y. YIDDISH (JEWISH-GERMAN) VERSIONS.**

BIBLIOGRAPHY: Hans Rost, *Die Bibel im Mittelalter,* 1939; Hermann Strathmann, "Ueber einige moderne deutsche Uebersetzungen und Bearbeitungen des Neuen Testaments," in *Theologische Blaettern* (1940), cols. 330 ff.; Wilhelm Michaelis, *Uebersetzungen, Konkordanzen und konkordante Uebersetzung des Neuen Testaments,* 1947; G. Eis, *Fruehneuhochdeutsche Bibeluebersetzungen; Texte von 1400–1600,* 1949.

J. GREEK VERSIONS, MODERN: Under the auspices of Olga, Queen of the Hellenes, a Modern Greek version of the Gospels was published at Athens in 1900. The ancient Greek text was printed in parallel columns. In the following year Professor Alexander Pallis published a frankly vernacular version of Matthew's Gospel in an Athenian newspaper (*The Acropolis*). What was felt to be undue license in his version aroused bitter hostility, which extended to Queen Olga's version. The populace connected the latter book with a supposed Panslavist conspiracy, and riots occurred in the streets of Athens. This agitation led to the prohibition of the use of any modern Greek version of the New Testament. The prohibition was repealed in 1924. Pallis' completed version of the Gospels (based on the Vatican codex, B) was published at Liverpool in 1902.

In 1946 K. Phrilingos published at Athens a new translation of the Psalms. The Professor of Old Testament at the University of Athens, B. Vellas, has begun publishing (Athens, 1947—)

a commentary on the Minor Prophets, which includes his own rendering of the Hebrew text into modern Greek. Instead of the usual "kyrios" of the Septuagint for the Hebrew tetragrammaton, Vellas uses a transliteration of Yahweh. Poetic passages are printed in strophes.

K. HEBREW TRANSLATIONS OF THE NEW TESTAMENT: J. M. P. Bauchet, O.C.D., has begun to revise Delitzsch's Hebrew New Testament (which in later editions was made to conform to the Greek *textus receptus*) on the basis of M. J. Lagrange's work in establishing a critical Greek text. Two editions of Matthew have been published (Jerusalem, 1950), one with and one without vowel points. Mark was issued with vowel points (1950).

BIBLIOGRAPHY: S. R. Driver, "Two Hebrew New Testaments (Delitzsch's and Salkinson's)," *Expositor*, Third Series, III (1886), 260–275. See also Y. YIDDISH VERSIONS.

L. HUNGARIAN (MAGYAR) VERSIONS: The revision of the Old Testament in the classic Károli version (1590), published in 1898, aroused so much adverse criticism that another committee, under the leadership of Elek Petri, undertook further revision in order to bring it into general accord with the English Revised Version. The work of this committee resulted in so many alterations of the time-honored text that many felt it to be misleading to call this a revision of the Károli translation. At the same time, many linguistic archaisms which were permitted to remain prevented the revision from gaining general acceptance.

Among several attempts to produce a more satisfactory translation, the following may be mentioned: In 1903 István Kecskeméthy published at Budapest his version of St. Mark's Gospel. A Jewish translation was prepared by an editorial committee of V. Bacher, J. Bánóczi, and S. Krausz, and published in four volumes (1898–1907), by the Jewish Hungarian Literary Society (Vols. 8, 12, 18, and 24 in its series). In 1923 Stefan Barcy, a former burgomaster of Budapest, published with ecclesiastical approbation his translation of the four Gospels. This was arranged in the form of a single narrative, ordered chronologically, in eleven chapters, having from one to twenty-one sections each. A revised and illustrated edition was published by the British and Foreign Bible Society (Budapest, 1935). Dr. Bernat Frenkel translated the Old Testament (Budapest, 1927). Aladár Hornyánszky translated Amos (printed in strophic form; Bratislava, 1936), as well as Job, Romans, I Thessalonians, and Hebrews. Ladislaus Farkas translated the Gospels and Acts (Debrecen, 1938).

It was, however, work by two representative scholars, Pastor Alexander Czeglédy of the Reformed Church of Hungary, and Bishop Alexander Raffay of the Lutheran Church, which laid the foundations for a revision which, it is hoped, will prove to be satisfactory to all Hungarian Protestants. In 1929 the Luther Society of Budapest published Raffay's translation of the New Testament. Next, the British and Foreign Bible Society published Czeglédy's version of the New Testament (Budapest, 1930). Czeglédy, aided by a certain Rabbi Klein, prepared a translation of the Old Testament, which was published with Raffay's version of the New Testament (Budapest, 1938). In 1943 the British and Foreign Bible Society authorized the publication in Hungary of a Bible with the 1938 Old Testament slightly revised by Czeglédy and with Czeglédy's rather than Raffay's translation of the New Testament. Because of increasing criticisms leveled against the work of these two outstanding scholars, who died during the war years, a Joint Bible Commission of the two representative Protestant churches was appointed in 1947, formed of seven Old Testament and seven New Testament scholars. Through a newly (1949) constituted Hungarian Bible Council of the Evangelical churches of Hungary, other Protestant Churches (Baptist, Methodist, Brethren, Adventists) also have a certain responsibility for the revision. The latest editions of Kittel's Hebrew Bible and of Nestle's Greek Testament form the textual basis, and a literal translation is attempted, avoiding the frequent euphemisms and paraphrases of the previous revisions, and retaining in modern Hungarian all that is still alive in the idiom of the Károli translation. Long sentences are broken up, and the orthography follows new official rules. Where the critical Greek text departs from the *textus receptus* (particularly in familiar passages) the variants are given in brackets or in notes. In the Old Testament the tetragrammaton is rendered by ÚR (Lord) in capital letters. The copious use of marginal references and explanatory notes (bearing upon the continuity of revelation and "saving history") resembles the old Károli Bible. A trial edition of Genesis appeared in 1951. The New Testament was completed in 1952.

BIBLIOGRAPHY: The introduction to the trial edition of Genesis (in English, German, and Hungarian); and Ladislaus M. Pákozdy, "The New Revision of the Hungarian Bible," in *Bulletin of the United Bible Societies*, No. 6 (1951), pp. 11-15. For the classical Vizsoly Bible, see the essays in the Festschrift in honor of its translator, Károli: *Károlyi Emlékkönyu . . .* , ed. Béla Vasady, 1940.

M. ICELANDIC VERSIONS. See **V. SCANDINAVIAN VERSIONS.**

N. ITALIAN VERSIONS: Most of the Italian translations made by Roman Catholic scholars are based on the Latin Vulgate, and all are provided with notes and comments. The S. Girolamo Society Version of the Gospels and Acts, prepared by P. Clementi, was published at Rome in 1902. Monsignor Antonio Martini's version, revised and corrected, appeared at Turin in 1920. The Compagnia di S. Paulo Version of the Bible was prepared by Giuseppi Ricciotti and a company of scholars and was published by the Cardinal Ferrari Society (Florence, 1929). Although based on the Vulgate, variations from the Hebrew and Greek are noted in the margin. In 1929 Giovanni Re, S.J., translated the Gospels from Vogels' Greek text. Marco Sales, O.P., Maestro del S. Palazzo Apostolico, published his rendering of the Vulgate at Turin in 1931. Dain Cohenel's translation appeared in parts (1930–33), at Gravina de Puglia. The "Bibbia di Firenze" under the care of the Pontifical Biblical Institute, directed by Alberto Vaccari, S.J., began to appear in 1922. It is in a modern, flowing, dignified, and simple Italian. The introduction and notes are brief and non-argumentative. The translators depart from the traditional text (Vulgate) only "when it is morally certain that the text is corrupt and what the original reading must have been." Another translation of the original texts with the Latin Vulgate printed opposite has appeared under the direction of S. Garofalo (Turin, 1948). Salvatore Quasimodo published his translation of John's Gospel (Milan, 1950) with the Greek text on the opposite page.

Among Protestant scholars Giovanni Luzzi (of the Waldensian theological faculty, Rome) has been the most active. He published his version of the New Testament at Rome in 1911, and of the Bible in 1930. He also headed a committee revising the old Diodati version; the New Testament was published by the British and Foreign Bible Society in 1916; the Bible in 1925. Subsequently, at the request of Seventh-day Adventists, the rendering of Rev. 1:10, "nel giorno della Domenica," was changed to "nel giorno del Signore."

O. LITHUANIAN AND LETTISH VERSIONS: In 1904 A. Eynars of Memel published at Berlin a revision of the New Testament in the Samogit dialect of Lithuanian. A reprint of J. A. Giedraitis' 1816 version, with orthographic changes, was published at Shenandoah, Pa., in 1906. It was edited by S. Pautienins, a Roman Catholic priest of Mahanoy City, Pa. Another Roman Catholic edition of the Bible in the Samogit dialect was prepared by Bishop Juozapas Skvireckas and was published in six volumes (Kaunas, 1922) as a memorial to the five hundredth anniversary of the Samogit Bishops (1421–1921).

In 1930 the Synod of the Reformed Church of Lithuania appointed Povalis Jakubenas and Adomas Sernas to prepare a revision of the New Testament. The Gospels were published at Memel in 1934, and the work on the New Testament was completed by A. Jurenas of Canada (British and Foreign Bible Society, *Popular Report* [1951], p. 82).

In 1898 R. Auning, a pastor at Sesswegen, and others appointed by the Evangelical Synods of Courland and Livonia, published at Riga a revision of the Lettish version of the Bible. This, with further revisions of the New Testament in accordance with Westcott and Hort's Greek text, was published at Leipzig in 1902. A translation of the Gospels by a committee of pastors was published by the British and Foreign Bible Society at Riga in 1933. This was the first edition to appear using roman characters. The New Testament was published in 1937.

BIBLIOGRAPHY: Paul Salopiata, *Das Verhaeltnis der Evangelien-Texte in den aeltesten katholisch-litauischen Drucken*, 1929.

P. NORWEGIAN VERSIONS. See **V. SCANDINAVIAN VERSIONS.**

Q. PERSIAN VERSIONS: A sixteenth century Persian Harmony of the Gospels, copied from a parent manuscript of the thirteenth century, throws new light on the history of the Gospels in Persia. The manuscript (edited by G. Messina) not only reveals many Tatianic readings, but also appears to be closely related to the Pococke manuscript which provides the Persian text in Walton's Polyglot Bible.

Fischel's study of the history of Bible translations in Persia reveals that the Pentateuch translation of Jacob ben Tarus (1546), so far from being, as has been long believed, the first and only such translation by Persian Jews, stands at the end of a long chain of Judaeo-Persian translations.

The most recent translation into modern Persian is the version of Wm. M. Miller and Ahmed, printed in Leipzig and published in Teheran by the Intermission Literature Committee: Acts (1932); Luke (1934); etc.

BIBLIOGRAPHY: Eduard Sachau, "Vom Christentum in der Persia," in *SBA*, phil.-hist. Kl., XXIX (1916), 971 ff; Giuseppe Messina, *Notizie su un Diatessaron persiano tradotta dal siriaco*, 1943; Bruce M. Metzger, "Tatian's Diatessaron and a Persian Harmony of the Gospels," *JBL*, LXIX (1950), 261–280; G. Messina, *Diatessaron persiano*, 1951; Walter J. Fischel, "The Bible in Persian Translation," *HTR*, XLV (1952), 3-45.

R. POLISH VERSIONS. See **W. SLAVIC VERSIONS.**

S. PORTUGUESE VERSIONS: In 1902 a group of Franciscans began to prepare a translation of the New Testament, publishing it in parts at Bahia, Brazil. Huberto Rohden, a Roman Catholic scholar with leanings toward theosophy, began to translate the New Testament while studying at Innsbruck in 1924–27, finishing it after returning to Brazil (Petropolis, 1934). Based on the Greek texts edited by Nestle and by Vogels, the rendering has been widely praised as clear, smooth, and esthetically agreeable. The third edition (1942) seems to have been revised according to Roesch's German version.

A revision of the d'Almeida version, designed especially for use in Brazil, was prepared by a committee of Brazilians and Protestant missionaries representing several denominations. The New Testament was published at Rio de Janeiro in 1910; the Bible in 1914; corrected edition, 1926. This Versão Brasileira, patterned largely upon the American Standard Version of 1901, has never been able to supplant the popular d'Almeida rendering. Beginning work in 1941, a commission of Baptist scholars published a rigorous revision of the d'Almeida New Testament (Rio de Janeiro, 1949), following the Nestle Greek text. In 1951 the Bible Society of Brazil published an "authorized revision" of the d'Almeida New Testament which seeks to preserve in modern orthography much of the familiar phraseology of the older rendering. A certain amount of information about variant readings in the Greek is given in footnotes. The revision of the Old Testament is expected to be ready by 1955.

T. ROMANY VERSIONS: Gypsies in Spain were the earliest of their race to possess a book of Scripture in their own tongue, Gitano or Spanish Romany. This was the Gospel of Luke translated in 1837 by George Borrow, then agent of the British and Foreign Bible Society at Madrid. A revised form was published at Madrid in 1872. Besides the Spanish form of Romany, some portion of Scripture now exists in no fewer than ten other forms of the Romany tongue, namely Central Bulgarian, South Eastern Bulgarian, North German, South German, Hungarian, Italian, Lettish, Moravian (spoken by approximately 50,000 gypsies in Czechoslovakia and Ukrainia), Scottish, and Yugoslav.

U. RUSSIAN VERSIONS. See **W. SLAVIC VERSIONS.**

V. SCANDINAVIAN VERSIONS: 1. DANISH VERSIONS: The translation of the New Testament by Bishop T. Skat Rördam (Copenhagen, 1886), which retained much of the traditional Danish Biblical language, was made from a Greek text established by modern scholarship. This translation became very popular. In 1897 another translation of the New Testament was published by Bishop A. S. Poulsen and J. L. Ussing. Frants Buhl, the famous Hebrew scholar of Copenhagen, with the assistance of other scholars, published a rendering of the Old Testament which departs frequently from the Masoretic text in preference for readings supported by ancient versions.

The current text is the 1907 revision of the New Testament and the 1931 revision of the Old Testament. This was prepared by a Royal Commission consisting of the most prominent Danish scholars, and has been authorized to be read in churches. In 1942 a "test revision" of the New Testament was issued, looking forward to an authorized revision.

2. ICELANDIC VERSIONS: In 1897 the Icelandic Bible Society made arrangements to revise thoroughly the version of Gudbrandur Thorláksson, Bishop of Hólar, which had been frequently reprinted, sometimes with minor revisions, since its first publication at Holum in 1584. Specimens of the revision of various Old and New Testament books were published. After consideration had been given to various criticisms, the complete Bible was published by the British and Foreign Bible Society at Reykjavik in 1908.

3. NORWEGIAN VERSIONS: Special linguistic changes within Norway have necessitated frequent revisions of the vernacular versions. After four centuries of union with Denmark, the official Norwegian written language had become quite Danish, and in the middle of the nineteenth century an effort was made to return to the genuine Norwegian language. A composite of various rural dialects was made and called *Landsmaal* or New Norwegian. Both the official Norwegian written language and New Norwegian have been becoming more like each other, and consequently translations of the Bible in each form of the language require frequent revision.

Noteworthy revisions include the following: Under the guidance of Professor H. J. M. A. Seippel, portions of the Scriptures have appeared in *Landsmaal;* the Gospels (Oslo, 1915–20); the Acts (1923); Samuel and Kings (1930). The Students' Folkemaal Society of Oslo published a translation of the Bible in 1921. A committee of two theologians (Alanaes and Messel) and two professors (Odland and Seippel) revised the Old Caspari version to make the language more Norwegian. This revision was published by the Norwegian Bible Society at Oslo in 1930. At the end of the Bible is a list of passages omitted by many manuscripts. In 1938 the Norwegian Bible Society published a revised version of the Bible in New Norwegian, prepared by Pastor R. Indrebö.

4. SWEDISH VERSIONS: At the end of the last century, O. F. Myrberg published at Stockholm his translation of the New Testament (1890) and of most of the Old Testament (1887–1899). A Roman Catholic version of the New Testament, translated by J. P. E. Benelius, was published at Stockholm in 1895. J. August Edman's scholarly rendering of the New Testament, printed at Göteborg, was published at Stockholm in 1900.

In 1773 Gustavus III appointed a Bible Commission of leading biblical scholars to revise the "Charles XII's Bible" of 1703. The revisers and their successors submitted many specimens of their work to the Church Diet, but none of them met with final approval until 1917. In that year a revision of the 1903 translation of the Old Testament and of the 1907 translation of the New Testament was finally accepted and recommended to the king for his authorization.

BIBLIOGRAPHY: O. M. Norlie, *The Translated Bible, 1534–1934* (1934), pp. 122–157; *Festskrift utgiven av teologiska fakulteten i Uppsala 1941 till 400-årsminnet av bibelns utgivande paa svenska,* 1941; R. Gyllenberg (ed.), *Vaara fäders Bibel 1541–1941. Minnesskrift utgiven av teologiska fakulteten vid Åbo akademi,* 1941; J. Lindblom and H. Pleijel, *Observationes Strengnenses,* 1943; B. Molde, *Källorna till Christian III:s Bibel 1550. Text filologiska studier i reformationstidens danska bibelöversättningar,* 1949; P. Otzen, *Hvorledes danskerne fik deres Bibler,* 1949; B. Molde (ed.), *Bidrag till den danske Bibels Historie. Festskrift in Anledning af den danske Bibels 400 Aars Jubilaeum,* 1950.

W. SLAVIC VERSIONS: 1. BOHEMIAN (CZECH) VERSIONS: F. Zilka, a pastor of the Evangelical Church of the Czech Brethren and professor on the Hus Theological Faculty, Prague, published his version of the New Testament at Prague in 1933. J. Hejčl's revision of J. L. Sykora's edition of the New Testament was published at Frýdek in 1946. Another translation of the New Testament by R. Col was issued at Velehrad in 1947.

Sporadic and superficial studies in the nature of the Old Bohemian version suggest that a complete knowledge of this text might yield results of much importance for the "Western" text (so J. H. Ropes, *The Text of Acts* [1926], p. cxli). For a résumé of various studies of this version, especially in relation to other Slavic versions, see Josef Vraštil, S.J., "Quomodo sacri codicia bohemici iubilaeum quingentorum annorum digne celebrandum sit; conspectus recentiorum de antiqua bibliorum versione bohemica litterarum et consilia," *Acta academiae velehradensis,* IX (1913), 31-44.

2. BULGARIAN VERSIONS: A revision of the New Testament, made by a committee headed by Robert Thomson, was published at Sofia in 1921; the Bible, in 1923. In 1891 a committee appointed by the Synod of the Bulgarian Orthodox Church, under the leadership of the Metropolitan Boris, Exarch of Bulgaria, began work on a version of the Scriptures. After five committees had worked successively on the project, the translation was published at Sofia in 1925.

3. OLD CHURCH SLAVONIC; see **I. Ancient Versions: M. OLD SLAVIC VERSION.**

4. POLISH VERSIONS: The Wujek version, which is the standard Roman Catholic Bible in Polish, was revised most recently in 1935. One of the best Protestant versions is that prepared by Jan Szersuda, a minister of the Lutheran Church in Poland. A translation of the New Testament was published by the Mariasite archbishop, O. J. M. Michal Kowalski (Plock, 1928).

5. RUSSIAN VERSIONS: Count Leo Nikolaevich Tolstoy drew up a Gospel Harmony (Geneva, 1890). In 1946 Joseph Schweigl, S.J., prepared a translation of the New Testament for the Russian Pontifical College of Rome to use in missionary work.

A translation of the New Testament and Psalms in White Russian, prepared by A. Luckiewicz and D. Malej, was published by the British and Foreign Bible Society at Helsingfors in 1931.

The Ukrainian (or Ruthenian) version of the Bible, translated by P. A. Kulisch, D. I. Puluj, I. C. Levitsky, and revised for printing by Alexander Sluszarczyk, was published in Russian characters at Vienna in 1903. Yaroslav Levitsky's translation of the New Testament, revised by a committee of professors and officials of the Orthodox Church, was published at Žolkief (near Lemberg) in 1921.

6. SERBIAN, CROATIAN, AND SLOVENIAN VERSIONS: Serbs, Croats, and Slovenes are united politically in Yugoslavia. The first two speak the same language; the last two, being Roman Catholic, use the Roman alphabet; the Serbs, being Orthodox, use the Cyrillic alphabet. Dr. Lujo Bakotić, a minister of high cabinet rank, published his revision of the Vuk-Daničić version of the New Testament (in Roman characters) at Belgrade in 1930; the Bible, 1933. His translation has been termed "inescapably lucid." Dimitri Stefanović, professor of New Testament exegesis at the University of Belgrade, published at Belgrade in 1934 his version of the New Testament (in Cyrillic characters).

Two revisions of the Slovenian Bible were made during the twentieth century. The British and Foreign Bible Society published Anton Chraska's version of the New Testament at Laibach in 1908; of the Bible, 1914. Dr. Antona Bonaventura Jegliča, Bishop of Ljubljana (Laibach) translated the New Testament (1929).

7. SLOVAK VERSIONS: Catholic Slovaks (not to be confused with the Slovenes), first received the Scriptures in their own tongue in the nineteenth century when Jiři Palkovič, a canon of Gran, translated the Latin Vulgate Bible (Gran, 1832). His version was replaced in 1926 by the work of the Vojtech Union. This version was translated by Ján Donoval and a group of Roman Catholic scholars, and was revised by Richard Oswald. The New Testament was published in 1913; the Bible in 1928.

A Lutheran pastor, Josef Rohaček, translated from the original languages first the New Testament, which the British and Foreign Bible Society published at Budapest in 1913, and later the complete Bible (Prague, 1936). In 1946 Stefan Žlatoš and Anton Jan Surjanský published their translation of the New Testament at Trnava.

X. SPANISH VERSIONS: The classic version of Cipriano de Valera (1602) has been frequently republished with minor revisions. The text of current editions was prepared in 1909 by J. B. Cabrera and C. Tornos. This is now being revised again by a committee of representatives from Spain and all parts of Latin America. The revision is not to be a heavy one, but such as will remove archaisms and crudities, without affecting the quality of this much-loved version.

In 1909 a Jesuit, Juan José de la Torre, published at Freiburg a Greek and Spanish edition of the New Testament, of which a third edition appeared in 1939.

The "Hispano-Americana" New Testament (Madrid, 1916) was produced by a committee of Spanish and South American translators meeting in Spain, who used the Nestle Greek text and sought to make available in a joint version the advances in knowledge of text and language expressed in the English Revised Version.

Guillermo Juenemann, a Roman Catholic whose theology approached that of Protestantism, published in 1928 at Concepción (Chile) an extremely literal translation of the New Testament in everyday Spanish. Its text is based on the early Greek manuscripts (B, *aleph*, A), and contains no notes favorable to Romanism.

A Jesuit, José J. Réboli, revised the old Amat version (1825) of the Gospels, taking into account modern critical editions of the Greek text (Buenos Aires, 1944).

The first complete translation of the Bible into Spanish from the original languages made by Roman Catholic scholars is that of Canon Eloíno Nácar Fuster and Alberto Colunga. This quite modern translation was prepared under the auspices and direction of the Pontifical University of Salamanca (Madrid, 1944; 4th ed., 1951). The notes specially related to passages which prohibit idolatry appear to be less defensive than those which occur in earlier Roman Catholic versions (e.g., the Scio San Miguel and the Amat versions).

In 1944 Monsignor Juan Straubinger began to publish the first Spanish version of the Greek Gospels made in America (Buenos Aires, 1944); Acts (1946); Romans to Hebrews (2 vols., 1948). His version is based on Merk's Greek text compared with Nestle's.

Francisco Cantera and José Maria Bover, S.J., published their version at Madrid in 1947. The Old Testament is based on Kittel's Hebrew Bible, and the New Testament on Bover's edition of the Greek text. The aim of the translators was to provide a rendering marked by fidelity to the original, clarity, and "hispanidad."

BIBLIOGRAPHY: C. W. Turner, *La Biblia en América Latina*, 1951.

Y. YIDDISH (JEWISH-GERMAN) VERSIONS: Yiddish is a conglomerate language based on Middle High German mixed with Hebrew (both biblical and postbiblical) and with varying elements of Slavic dialects of Lithuania, Poland, Bessarabia, etc., depending upon the locality of the speakers. The first publication of the New Testament (without the Book of Revelation) appeared at Cracow in 1540, translated by Johann Harzuge. The Old Testament, translated by Jekuthiel ben Isaac Blitz and revised by Meir Stern, was published at Amsterdam in 1676–78. Subsequently, besides the translation of parts of the Scriptures (which are not mentioned here), the New Testament was translated by Christian Moeller (Frankfurt a.d. Oder, 1700), and by Johann Heinrich Reitz (Offenbach, 1703).

The Old Testament was translated by Naphtali Hirz b. Suesskind and Menahem b. Solomon Levi (Amsterdam, 1725–29). In 1732 J. H. Callenberg published at Halle his translation of the New Testament. The New Testament in rabbinic characters, translated by Benjamin Nehemiah Solomon, was published by the London Jews Society (London, 1821). P. I. Hershon's translation of the New Testament (London, 1878) was revised by J. Rabinowitz, W. I. Nelom, and Joseph Lerner (Berlin, 1901) in an attempt to combine Lithuanian, Bessarabian, and Galician forms. J. A. Adler published his translation of the New Testament at London in 1895. In 1908 the British and Foreign Bible Society published the Bible translated by Mordecai Samuel Bergmann of the London City Mission and revised by Aaron Bernstein of the London Jews Society. The New Testament was revised again in 1912 by Bergmann, Bernstein, A. S. Geden, S. H. Wilkinson, and R. Kilgour, and the Old Testament in 1927. C. Neuhausen, A. H. Charlap, and others edited the Hebrew of the Old Testament with a Yiddish translation on opposite pages (4 vols., New York, 1919). Solomon Bloomgarden (under the pseudonym Jehoash) published his translation of the Old Testament (New York, 1926–36).

A fresh problem relating to Yiddish Scriptures grows out of the inevitable linguistic modification of the language of Central European Jews who have migrated to English speaking countries, particularly the United States, where gradually English words and idioms have supplanted certain Yiddish expressions. Henry Einspruch attempted to meet this problem with his *American Translation of the New Testament into the Yiddish Language* (Brooklyn, 1941). See also **K. HEBREW TRANSLATIONS OF THE NEW TESTAMENT.**

BIBLIOGRAPHY: W. Staerk and A. Lietzmann, *Die Juedisch-Deutschen Bibeluebersetzungen von den Anfaengen bis zum Ausgang des 18. Jahrhunderts*, 1923; S. Noble, "Sacred and Secular in the Language of the Yiddish Bible Translation," in *Yivo Annual of Jewish Social Science*, I (1946), 274-282.

Z. BIBLE VERSIONS FOR THE MISSION FIELD: See article, MISSION FIELD, BIBLE VERSIONS FOR THE. [Sup.] BRUCE M. METZGER.

VII

SEPTUAGINT: Originally the term "Septuagint" (LXX) was applied to the Greek Pentateuch, which probably was translated in the reign of Ptolemy Philadelphus (285–246 B.C.). The exact origin of this version is uncertain and encrusted with legend. As regards the number seventy, it may be an approximation for seventy-two, or it may have developed traditionally (for seventy, cf. the elders in Ex. 24:1, 9; the membership of the Sanhedrin; the generally accepted reading, Luke 10:1, 17; see M. Hadas, *Aristeas to Philocrates* [*Letter of Aristeas*], 1951). From Aristeas we infer that in its final form the Greek Pentateuch was the product of editorial harmonization. Probably by 150 B.C. most of the Old Testament existed in Greek, and eventually the name LXX was applied to the entire Greek Old Testament previous to revision or new translations; it would be more accurate to speak of the Old Greek version, but the term LXX is well established in this restricted sense. Naturally the style varies in different books, and the version is of unequal merit (cf. H. S. Gehman, "The Septuagint" under "Versions" in *Westminster Dictionary of the Bible* [1944]).

Considerable research has been done on the LXX since 1908. (For the division of labor among the translators of certain books, see H. St. J. Thackeray, *The Septuagint and Jewish Worship* [Schweich Lectures], 1923.) P. E. Kahle (*Th. St. u. Kritiken*, Vol. 88 [1915], pp. 410–426; *The Cairo Geniza* [Schweich Lectures], 1947), on his interpretation of Aristeas, maintains that there were earlier translations of the Pentateuch, of which a revision was made in the time of Ptolemy; this then became the standard Greek Torah. For the other books of the Old Testament he also postulates independent Greek renderings; when the church needed a canonical text of the entire Old Testament, it took one form of the various texts and with revision adapted it for Christian readers. In other words, he does not believe that there was one original Old Greek version, and consequently the manuscripts of the LXX would not go back essentially to one archetype. (In this connection cf. T. W. Manson's review of Kahle's *The Cairo Geniza* in *Dominican Studies,* Vol. II [1949], pp. 183–192; and E. J. Bickerman, "Some Notes on the Transmission of the Septuagint," in *Alexander Marx Jubilee Volume,* Eng. Section [1950], 149–178.) This is in contrast to P. de Lagarde, who saw the problems involved and the correct methodology for recovering the text of the original LXX. He was followed by A. Rahlfs, whose *Septuaginta Studien,* 3. Heft, appeared in 1911, and *Septuaginta, Genesis,* in 1926; he is also the editor of a complete text, *Septuaginta, id est V. T. Graece iuxta LXX Interpretes* (Stuttgart, 1935). A thoroughgoing attempt at establishing the text of one LXX book on Lagardian principles was made by M. L. Margolis, *The Book of Joshua in Greek* (1931), parts 1–4 (chaps. 1—19:38); he maintains that the text "as it appears at the top of the page is the nearest approach to the Greek original as it left the hands of the translator(s)." The methods initiated by Lagarde were successfully applied by J. A. Montgomery in two commentaries in the *ICC: Daniel* (1927); and *Kings* (1951). For an appreciation of Lagardian principles and extensive bibliography on LXX work in general, see H. M. Orlinsky, "On the Present State of Proto-Septuagint Studies," in *JAOS,* 61 (1941), 81–91; *idem.,* "The Septuagint—Its Use in Textual Criticism," in *Biblical Archaeologist,* 9 (1946); *idem.,* "Current Progress in Septuagint Research" in H. R. Willoughby (ed.), *The Study of the Bible Today and Tomorrow* (1947); *idem.,* "Margolis' Work in the Septuagint" in *Max Leopold Margolis, Scholar and Teacher* (a memorial volume) (1952). In this volume J. Reider also presents a complete bibliography of the writings of that LXX scholar. In defense of Lagarde's principles and the work of Rahlfs, cf. P. Katz, "Das Problem des Urtextes der Septuaginta," in *TZ,* V (1949), 1–24; "Recovery of Original LXX—A Study in the History of Transmission and Text. Criticism," in *Actes du Premier Congrès de la Féd. Int. des Assoc. d'Études Classiques* (1951), 165–182.

It is now well known that Hebrew texts in Greek transcription were used by Jews; an example of such a text is the second column of the Hexapla. F. Wutz advanced the theory that the LXX was rendered from a Hebrew text written in Greek characters: *Die Transkriptionen von der Septuaginta bis zu Hieronymus* (1925–33). A great deal of research was expended on this volume of 571 pages to prove his hypothesis, but it has not been accepted by scholars.

From Egypt the LXX spread to all parts of the Hellenistic Jewish world, and in course of time different text traditions developed in centers like Alexandria, Caesarea, and Antioch. The possibility of pre-recensional revisions on the basis of local Hebrew texts must in this connection receive serious consideration. The LXX became the Old Testament of the Christians, who used it in their controversies with the

Jews, even though it differed in various words or passages from the Hebrew text then in vogue. Accordingly need arose for another translation or new renderings of the Old Testament. This brings us to "the Three," of whom Theodotion probably comes first in time. He did not produce a new version, but apparently worked on a tradition current in Asia Minor, which is referred to by biblical scholars as Ur-Theodotion or pre-Theodotion (cf. Montgomery, *op. cit.;* Kahle, *Die Heb. Handschriften aus d. Hoehle* [1951], p. 33). In connection with the three main recensions of the Greek Bible some attention must be given to the background of Lucian's text. The appearance of Lucianic readings preceding Lucian (martyred A.D. 311/12) along with their occurrence in Old Latin texts has raised complicated problems still unsolved, and accordingly an Ur-Lucian or a pre-Lucianic version native to Antioch and Syria has been postulated (cf. Montgomery, *op. cit.;* Kahle, *op. cit.,* p. 34).

The LXX represents a pre-Masoretic Hebrew text and accordingly is important for textual and exegetical studies. The methods of translation, however, should also be observed; frequently extreme literalism and freedom of rendering are found in the same verse or adjacent verses. Also certain definite exegetical principles were employed by the translators; for theological reasons some expressions concerning God, which were regarded as crude or offensive, were softened down, and anthropomorphisms were frequently removed. In many cases the end was achieved by the trick of the translator, in which he played with the Hebrew roots. Yet the translators did not set out to rewrite the original, and these exegetical principles which show a theological tendency were not consistently carried out (cf. C. T. Fritsch, *The Anti-Anthropomorphisms of the Greek Pentateuch,* 1943; H. S. Gehman, "The Theological Approach of the Greek Translator of Job 1–15," in *JBL,* 68 [1949], 231–240; *idem,* "Exegetical Methods Employed by the Greek Translator of I Samuel," in *JAOS,* 70 [1950], 292–296; D. H. Gard, *The Exegetical Method of the Greek Translator of the Book of Job,* J. B. L. Monograph Series, Vol. VIII, 1952; J. W. Wevers, "Principles of Interpretation Guiding the Fourth Translator of the Book of the Kingdoms [3 K. 22:1—4 K. 25:30]," in *Cath. Bibl. Q.,* 14 [1952], 40–56; "A Study in the Exegetical Principles Underlying the Greek Text of 2 Sam. 11:2—1 Kings 2:11," in *ibid.,* 15 [1953], 30–45). The LXX accordingly cannot be used in a merely mechanical manner to emend the Masoretic text.

Under linguistic studies of LXX Greek should be mentioned H. St. J. Thackeray, *A Grammar of the Old Testament in Greek according to the Septuagint* (1909); H. S. Gehman, "The Hebraic Character of Septuagint Greek," in *Vetus Testamentum,* I (1951), 81–90; *idem,* "Hebraisms of the Old Greek Version of Genesis," *ibid.,* III (1953), 141–148. In connection with the Greek Old Testament should also be noted J. Reider, *Prolegomena to a Greek-Hebrew and Hebrew-Greek Index to Aquila* (1916); J. H. Moulton, *Grammar of New Testament Greek,* Vol. I (3d ed., 1908); *idem,* with W. F. Howard, *ibid.,* Vol. II (1929). This grammar has many references to the LXX and an appendix on Semitisms in the New Testament.

An indispensable handbook to LXX studies is H. B. Swete, *An Introduction to the Old Testament in Greek,* revised by R. R. Ottley (1914). For manuscripts and versions cf. F. G. Kenyon, *The Text of the Greek Bible* (1937); *idem, Our Bible and the Ancient Manuscripts* (4th ed., 1939). A general work on the LXX is R. R. Ottley, *A Handbook to the Septuagint* (1920). According to H. M. Orlinsky the Tetrapla was not a separate edition of Origen's critical work with the omission of the two Hebrew columns of the Hexapla, but the term was loosely used for the Hexapla when the four Greek columns (Tetrapla) were stressed rather than all six (Hexapla); cf. "Origen's Tetrapla—a Scholarly Fiction?" in *World Congress of Jewish Studies, Summer of 1947* (1952), 173–182.

Among Greek papyri of the Old Testament should be noted fragments of Deut. 23:24(26)—24:3; 25:1–3; 26:12, 17–19; 28:31–33 of the second century B.C. It is important that this text agrees with A and Theodotion rather than with B; for these texts cf. C. H. Roberts, *Two Biblical Papyri in the John Rylands Library Manchester* (1936). The Chester Beatty Papyri, dating variously from the first half of the second, the third, and the fourth centuries A.D., contain portions of Genesis, Numbers, Deuteronomy, Isaiah, Jeremiah, Ezekiel, Daniel, Esther, and Ecclesiasticus; cf. F. G. Kenyon, *The Chester Beatty Biblical Papyri;* fasc. 4 (1934); 5 (1935); 6 (1937); 7 (1937). The John H. Scheide Biblical Papyri of forty-two pages, which contain, with some losses, Ezek. 19:12—39:29, are dated in the early third century and come from the same codex as the Chester Beatty Papyrus of this book (Kenyon IX; Rahlfs and Ziegler no. 967). They have been published in photographic reproduction and transcription with critical apparatus, introductory chapters, and notes under the editorship of A. C. Johnson, H. S. Gehman, and E. H. Kase (1938); cf. also H. S. Gehman, "Relations between Heb. Text of Ezek. and Sch. Papyri," in *JAOS,* 58 (1938), 92–102; *idem,* "Rel. between Text of Sch. Pap. and that of other Gr. Mss. of Ezek.," in *JBL,* 57 (1938), 281–287; J. Ziegler, "Die Bedeutung der C. Beatty-Scheide Pap. 967 . . . Ezech.-Septuaginta," in *ZAW,* 61 (1945–48), 76–94. See also PAPYRI, BIBLICAL AND EARLY CHRISTIAN.

In addition to the editions of the LXX of

Swete and Rahlfs there is the large Cambridge edition of *The Old Testament in Greek* begun under the editorship of A. E. Brooke and N. McLean. Vol. I: *The Octateuch* was published in 4 parts (1906–17). The same scholars together with H. St. J. Thackeray edited Vol. II: *The Later Historical Books* (Samuel, Kings, Chronicles, Esdras, and Ezra-Nehemiah), which appeared in 4 parts (1927–35). Vol. III, part 1 (Esther, Judith, Tobit), edited by the same three men, was published in 1940. The present editor of this work is T. W. Manson of Manchester University.

Another important edition of the LXX with an extensive critical apparatus is the *Septuaginta, Vetus Testamentum Graecum* (*Auctoritate Societatis Litterarum Gottingensis editum*); cf. P. L. Hedley, "The Goettingen Investigation and Edition of the LXX," in *HTR*, XXVI (1933), 57–72. The following have appeared (Goettingen) to date: Vol. IX, I: *I Maccabees*, ed. W. Kappler (1936); Vol. X: *Psalms with the Odes*, ed. A. Rahlfs (1931) (cf. rev. by O. Eissfeldt in *TLZ*, Vol. LVII [1932], pp. 153–155); Vol. XIII: *Twelve Minor Prophets* (1943); Vol. XIV: *Isaiah* (1939); Vol. XVI, 1: *Ezekiel* (1952); Vol. XVI, 2: *Susanna, Daniel, Bel et Draco* (1954); the last four publications have been edited by J. Ziegler.

See also BIBLE VERSIONS, I, D.

BIBLIOGRAPHY: In addition to the references throughout the article, see J. W. Wevers, "Septuaginta-Forschungen," *Theologische Rundschau*, N.F. XXII (1954), 85–137, 171–190.

[Sup.] HENRY S. GEHMAN.

VIII

HARMONY OF THE GOSPELS (TATIAN'S): In 1935 there was published a tiny parchment fragment of Tatian's Diatessaron in Greek, thus putting to an end the long debate whether or not Tatian's Harmony ever existed in Greek. The following translation of this fragment, discovered among the debris used in fortifying the Roman garrison city, Dura, on the Euphrates, just prior to its fall to the Persians under King Shapur I in A.D. 256–257, will give an idea of Tatian's painstaking attention to details in making a cento of all the distinctive elements of the four Gospels. (The restorations are enclosed within square brackets, and Scripture references—which are not, of course, in the fragment—are enclosed within parentheses.)

"[. . . the mother of the sons of Zebed]ee (Matt. 27:56) and Salome (Mark 15:40) and the wives [of those who] had followed him from [Galile]e to see the crucified (Luke 23:49b–c). And [the da]y was Preparation; the Sabbath was daw[ning] (Luke 23:54). And when it was evening (Matt. 27:57), on the Prep[aration], that is, the day before the Sabbath (Mark 15:42), [there came] up a man (Matt. 27:57), be[ing] a member of the Council (Luke 23:50), from Aramathea (Matt. 27:57), a city of Judea (Luke 23:51), by name Jo[seph] (Matt. 27:57), good and ri[ghteous] (Luke 23:50), being a disciple of Jesus, but se[cret]ly, for fear of the [Jew]s (John 19:38). And he (Matt. 27:57) was looking for [the] kingdom of God (Luke 23:51b). This man [had] not [con]sented to [their] p[urpose . . .] (Luke 23:51a)" (translated from C. H. Kraeling's edition in *Studies and Documents,* III, 1935).

Perhaps the most interesting variant reading preserved only in this fragment is the reference (based, it is true, partly on a restoration) to "the wives [of those who] had followed" Jesus from Galilee.

Secondary and tertiary witnesses to Tatian's Diatessaron are the following:

I. Eastern Witnesses: (1) The Syriac commentary on the Diatessaron by Ephraem (fourth century), preserved in an Armenian translation extant in two manuscripts (re-edited and translated by Louis Leloir [1954]); (2) an Arabic Diatessaron made from the Syriac and extant in two forms (A. S. Marmardji, ed.; see also A. J. B. Higgins, in *JTS,* Vol. XLX [1944], pp. 187–199; Georg Graf, *Geschichte der christlichen arabischen Literatur,* Vol. I [*Studi e Testi,* 118 (1944)], pp. 152–154; Paul Kahle, *The Cairo Geniza* [1947], pp. 197 ff.); (3) a Syriac Diatessaric lectionary for Passiontide extant in about twenty-five manuscripts (see appendix in Marmardji, *op. cit.,* pp. 1*–75*; also D. Willy in *Expository Times,* Vol. XXV [1913–14], pp. 31–35); (4) a medieval Persian Harmony of the Gospels made from a Syriac base (Giuseppe Messina, ed., *Diatessaron Persiano,* 1951), which contains also certain influence from the Protoevangelium of James; (5) evidence in various Syriac and Armenian Church Fathers, e.g., Aphraates, the *Liber Graduum,* Agathangelos, Eznik, etc., as well as the Armenian Breviary and Ritual (see St. Lyonnet, *Les origines de la version arménienne et le Diatessaron,* 1950), and Coptic Manichaean fragments (Polotsky and Allberry, eds.).

II. Western Witnesses: (6) the Codex Fuldensis (sixth century); (7) various medieval German Harmonies; (8) Middle Dutch (Flemish) Harmonies, the best known of which is the Liège Manuscript (Daniel Plooij, C. A. Phillips, and A. H. A. Bakker, eds., parts I–V, 1929–38); (9) two Old Italian Harmonies, one in the Tuscan dialect preserved in twenty-four manuscripts, the other in the Venetian dialect preserved in one manuscript (V. Todesco, A. Vaccari, and M. Vattasso, eds., *Il Diatessaron in volgare italiano,* 1938); (10) a Middle English Harmony which once belonged to Samuel Pepys (Margery Goates, ed., *The Pepysian Gospel Harmony,* 1927); (11) the harmonized Gospel text on which Zacharias Chrysopolitanus (Zachary of Besançon) wrote a commentary, early twelfth century (Migne, *PL,* CLXXXVI, cols. 11–620).

Not long after the Dura fragment was published another leaf (to be dated from the fifth or sixth century), believed to be from the Greek Diatessaron, was edited by Otto Stegmueller (*ZNTW,* Vol. XXXVII [1938], pp. 223–229). Further research, however, has not supported the original editor's belief, and Curt Peters has argued convincingly that at most this fragment reveals the influence of Tatian's Diatessaron in its variant readings (*Biblica,* Vol. XXI, [1940], pp. 51–55). The selections from Matthew and John which Agnes Smith Lewis published as "Fragments of a Greek Harmony of the Gospels" (in *Codex Climaci Rescriptus* [1909], xxvii-xxx) were drawn up in accord with a different plan from that of Tatian's Diatessaron.

A critical comparison of the sources mentioned above reveals the following characteristic details which scholars believe were present in the original Diatessaron. Several of these are noticeably colored by Tatian's Encratite leanings. (1) The account of light or fire seen at the baptism of Jesus; (2) the Davidic descent of Mary; (3) avoidance of reference to Joseph as the husband of Mary; (4) avoidance of reference to Joseph as Jesus' father; (5) the reduction of the married life of Hannah the prophetess to seven days; (6) the modification of the diet of John the Baptist to milk and honey; (7) transfer from God to Adam of the statement that a man and his wife shall be one flesh; (8) the addition of "with a rope" to the account of Judas' having hanged himself.

BIBLIOGRAPHY: The literature is very extensive. The best recent monograph is: Curt Peters, *Das Diatessaron Tatians; seine Ueberlieferung und sein Nachwirken im Morgen- und Abendland, sowie der heutige Stand seiner Erforschung,* 1939. Subsequent studies include: C. C. Torrey, *Documents of the Primitive Church,* (1941), pp. 271–295; C. Peters, "Die Entstehung der griechischen Diatessaron-uebersetzung und ihr Nachhall in byzantinischen Kirchen-poesie," in *Orientalia christiana periodica,* VIII (1942), 468–476; A. J. B. Higgins, "Tatian's Arabic Diatessaron" (summary, Ph.D. dissertation), in *Journal of the Manchester University Egyptian and Oriental Society,* XXIV (1942–45), 28–32; Matthew Black, *An Aramaic Approach to the Gospels and Acts* (1946), pp. 220–230; A. F. J. Klijn, *A Survey of the Researches into the Western Text of the Gospels and Acts* (dissertation, Utrecht, 1949), pp. 87–110; B. M. Metzger, "Tatian's Diatessaron and a Persian Harmony of the Gospels," in *JBL,* LXIX (1950), 261–280; Johannes Quasten, *Patrology,* Vol. I (1950), pp. 224–228; C. S. C. Williams, *Alterations to the Text of the Synoptic Gospels and Acts* (1951), pp. 19–24; B. M. Metzger, *Annotated Bibliography of the Textual Criticism of the New Testament, 1914–1939* (1955), pp. 73–81.

[Sup.] BRUCE M. METZGER.

IX

MISSION FIELD, BIBLE VERSIONS FOR THE: By A.D. 1450, before the era of printing, part or all of the Scriptures had been translated and published in thirty-three languages. By the end of the eighteenth century the Bible or portions of it had been printed in seventy-one languages. During the "missionary century" (the nineteenth) another 494 languages received something of the Bible, and by the middle of the twentieth century Scriptures had been published in another 560 languages. These publications represent Bibles in 191 languages and New Testaments in 246 other languages. The rest have one or more books, or in a few instances the equivalent thereof. The principal responsibility for publication of these Scriptures has rested with the Bible societies. The translation work has been largely the responsibility of the various missionary boards.

One of the very significant features of the modern missionary movement has been the ever increasing interest in translating the Bible into foreign languages. The languages into which Scriptures have now been translated represent about one half of the languages of the world which are spoken by approximately 90% of the world's population. There are, however, at least one thousand languages which as yet have nothing of the Bible, and the total population of these peoples is somewhat more than the population of all of North America. Missionary interest in reaching these additional one thousand groups is increasingly more manifest, especially as missionaries become more aware of the significance of Christian literature as a means of evangelism and become convinced of the value of adult literacy programs.

It must be noted, however, that interest in translations into new languages is even surpassed by concern for further translations in languages which already have something. Revisions of already existing translations also figure very extensively in missionary planning. By the middle of the twentieth century more Bible revision work was being undertaken than at any other time in the history of Christendom. The demand for revisions has reflected: (1) a greater awareness of textual criticism and hence of the existence of better and more reliable readings; (2) the recognition of more valid linguistic principles of translating, which result in more idiomatic renderings and greater intelligibility; (3) the realization, especially by second-generation Christians, that many of the earlier "missionary translations" are inadequate, both linguistically and textually; and (4) the availability of adequately trained native speakers who can undertake the leadership in preparing more widely acceptable versions. Revisions have not only been undertaken in such missionary languages as Siamese, Japanese, Tswa, and Malay, but also in German, English, Spanish, and Portuguese. At a conservative estimate it may be stated that at least five hundred missionaries and national workers are engaged principally or wholly in the task of Bible translating.

It has become more and more apparent that there is a great need for Bible translators to share their accumulated experience and to have additional helps which would guide them in their work. In 1947 the American Bible Society published *Bible Translating* as a textbook covering some of the more significant and important problems. It also prepared for the use of translators numerous helps in the form of check lists for analyzing the consistency in the use of words and the translating of parallel passages. Growing out of the report of a conference of translators, held in 1947 in Woudschoten, Holland, under the auspices of the Netherlands Bible Society, the United Bible Societies began in 1950 to publish *The Bible Translator,* a quarterly designed chiefly for Bible translators throughout the world (address: Netherlands Bible Society, Herengracht 366, Amsterdam—C).

BIBLIOGRAPHY: Eugene A. Nida, *Bible Translating,* 1947; Edwin W. Smith, *The Shrine of a People's Soul,* rev. ed., 1947; Violet Wood, *Great is the Company,* 1947; *Bulletin of the United Bible Societies,* quarterly beginning January, 1950; Eugene A. Nida, *God's Word in Man's Languages,* 1952.

[Sup.] EUGENE A. NIDA.

X

BIBLES, ANNOTATED: Only those annotated Bibles are included in which the English text of the whole Bible is presented. Unless otherwise noted the text is the King James Version.

Analytical Holy Bible, edited and arranged by A. Roberts. Egyptian Publishing Co., Carbondale, Ill., 1906.

The Modern Reader's Bible (English Revised Version) in modern literary form. Edited with introduction and notes by Richard G. Moulton, Macmillan, New York, 1907.

The Student's Bible, with marginal and explanatory footnotes and references, by Orville J. Nave and Anna S. Nave, Abingdon Press, New York, 1907, and republished since in seventy-nine editions.

The Marginal Chain-Reference Bible, compiled and edited by Frank Charles Thompson. Chain Reference Bible Publishing Co., Mt. Morris, N. Y., 1908, and reissued in 1917 (Eaton and Mains, New York), and in 1934 (Kirkbride Bible Co., Indianapolis, Ind.).

The Scofield Reference Bible. Topical references with annotations, edited by C. I. Scofield and seven consulting editors. Oxford University Press, New York, 1909; new and improved ed., 1917.

The Self-Interpreting Bible. A new edition with John Brown's notes. Introduction by John H. Vincent. Bible Educational Society, St. Louis, Mo., 1909.

The Cross-Reference Bible. American Standard Version, with variorum renderings and readings, topical analyses, and cross-references. Edited by Harold E. Monser. Cross-Reference Bible Co., New York, 1910.

The New Indexed Bible, comprising biblical biography, geography, history, teaching. John A. Dickson Publishing Co., Chicago, 1913. Also issued in 1923 and 1941.

The Companion Bible. With structures and notes; critical, expository, and suggestive. Six volumes. Oxford University Press, New York, 1909–21. New one volume edition in 1953.

Wilmore's New Analytical Reference Bible. Comprehensive helps, revised and edited between 1891 and 1918 by Philip Schaff. A complete analysis of the Holy Bible, edited by Roswell D. Hitchcock. Cruden's Concordance, revised by John Eadie. Funk & Wagnalls Co., New York, 1921.

The Bible for Today. With introductory paragraphs, headlines, and footnotes, by John Stirling. Illustrated by Rowland Hilder. Introduction by William Lyon Phelps. Oxford University Press, New York, 1941.

The Concordia Bible. Edited by John Theodore Mueller, with notes, introductions, explanations, instructions, and references. Concordia Publishing House, St. Louis, Mo., 1943.

The Westminster Study Edition of the Holy Bible. Paragraphed. Introductory articles and prefaces with footnotes, concordance, and maps. The Westminster Press, Philadelphia, 1948.

The Pilgrim Edition of the Holy Bible. With notes especially adapted for young Christians. Edited by E. Schuyler English. Oxford University Press, New York, 1948.

The Interpreter's Bible. With the King James and Revised Standard Version, and with general articles, as well as introduction, exegesis, and exposition for each book of the Bible. Edited by G. A. Buttrick and others. Twelve volumes. Abingdon-Cokesbury Press, New York, 1951–

BIBLIOGRAPHY: Readers who desire a more complete list are referred to the *Historical Catalogue of the Printed Editions of Holy Scripture,* in the Library of the British and Foreign Bible Society, compiled by T. H. Darlow and H. F. Moule, 2 vols., 1903 (a new edition of this catalogue is in preparation); *A Catalogue of Books Represented by Library of Congress Printed Cards,* issued to July 31, 1942, Vol. 14 (1943), pp. 1–255; *British Museum General Catalogue of Printed Books,* Vol. 16 (1936), Vol. 17 (1937), Vol. 18 (1937).

[Sup.] HOWARD TILLMAN KUIST.

APPENDIX

A

HEBREW LANGUAGE AND LITERATURE: Hebrew, the language in which almost the whole of the Old Testament was written, is a branch of the Semitic linguistic family (see SEMITIC LANGUAGES). Until forty years ago there were, to all intents and purposes, but few ancient Hebrew manuscripts, few documents in Hebrew outside the Bible. Today we can list some hundreds of early Hebrew inscriptions belonging to the first half of the first millenium B.C.

A significant find was made at Samaria in 1908. This comprised some eighty ostraca, or inscribed potsherds, belonging to the eighth century B.C. These proved to be invoices of oil and wine, the writing being in ink in a beautiful cursive style of the early Hebrew script. Here, indeed, were samples of the dialect and current hand of the Northern Kingdom of Israel.

During the last fifteen years there have become available two new sources of paramount importance for our knowledge of biblical Hebrew. The first were the twenty-one letters and other documents from Lachish (Southern Palestine), which were discovered in 1935 and 1938. They are written in ink in a bold current hand in perfect biblical Hebrew, with interesting idiomatic and orthographic features. They date to the early sixth century B.C., i.e., the period of Jeremiah. Together with the Siloam inscription they reflect the southern Judaean dialect of Hebrew, the classical language of the Old Testament. The philological importance of this and other new material has been considerable in several directions, e.g., in textual criticism, in the knowledge of Hebrew personal names, in historical-religious problems, etc. Perhaps of highest importance is the fact that the scholar of today has at his disposal a much broader and more detailed conspectus of the linguistic milieu of the biblical records.

The second, and more recent, source is furnished by the remarkable discovery in 1947 of the Dead Sea Scrolls (*q.v.*). In a cave near the northwestern end of the Dead Sea were discovered eleven leather manuscripts including hitherto unknown books, a scroll and a fragmentary scroll containing the text of Isaiah, and other items. As yet, there is no unanimity of opinion as to the exact date of these documents. The writer prefers the theory, held by many eminent scholars, that they belong to the second or first century B.C. The debate will no doubt continue for some considerable time. Nevertheless, it could in the meantime be said that the importance of these documents for our knowledge of Hebrew language and literature is paramount.

Hebrew was spoken and written in Palestine for more than a thousand years. After the fifth century B.C. it was gradually supplanted by Aramaic, but it is erroneous to think that it ever died out. Actually, it continued to be employed in "national" circles, and as the language of religious literature and poetry. In time a new form was developed, known as Mishnaic Hebrew. Even in later times, in the Middle and Modern Ages, Hebrew has never ceased to be current among Jews. This is evidenced by the vast Talmudic literature of the early Christian centuries, the *piyyutim,* or liturgical poems, composed in the sixth to the eleventh centuries, many of which survived in the Jewish prayer books, also by the numerous works of medieval Jewish scholars, poets, and philosophers, particularly of Spain, France, Italy, and Germany. Hebrew has, of course, remained the language of the synagogues, of the Jewish prayers, and of the Jewish religious schools. It was also the lingua franca and the language of correspondence of Jewish scholars of all ages and all countries. Since the late nineteenth century there has developed a flourishing modern Hebrew literature. The rebirth of Hebrew as a living language is one striking result of the development of Zionism. Its re-establishment as the language of the country in the new State of Israel is a striking fact. Indeed, spiritual and practical considerations have combined to associate the return of the Jews to Palestine with the return to Hebrew as their mother tongue.

BIBLIOGRAPHY: H. Bauer and P. Leander, *Historische Grammatik der hebraeischen Sprache,* 1918–22; G. Bergstraesser, *Hebraeische Grammatik,* 29th ed., W. Gesenius, 2 vols., 1918–29; H. Torczyner, *The Lachish Letters,* 1938; L. Koehler and W. Baumgartner, *Lexicon in Veteris Testamenti Libros,* 1948– ; M. Burrows, J. C. Trever and W. H. Brownlee (eds.), *The Dead Sea Scrolls of St. Mark's Monastery,* 1950.

[Sup.] DAVID DIRINGER.

B

HELLENISTIC GREEK: The extensive discoveries of new materials within the last half century have greatly increased our knowledge of Hellenistic Greek. Most important have continued to be the non-literary papyri (*q.v.*), ostraca, inscriptions, etc., publications of which have been legion. An important resource has also been the literary *koine* of such prose writers as Polybius, Diodorus, and Arrian; and modern Greek, in its spoken form a lineal descendant of the *koine,* has been exploited with valuable results. The findings of research have been helpfully integrated into new treatments of the history of the Greek language such as those of Norden (4th ed., 1923), Meillet (3rd ed., 1930) and Costas (1936), as well as into grammatical works. The important modern Greek studies initiated at the turn of the century have been carried forward in significant fashion by Pernot and others.

In lexicography (see Lexicons of the Greek New Testament) the new Liddell and Scott (completed 1940) includes the usage of papyri and early Christian "non-theological" literature. The new data have also been incorporated in several New Testament lexicons, from the brief works of Souter and Ebeling to the more extensive of Abbott-Smith, Zorell, Bauer, and Kittel. Special contributions have come from Moulton and Milligan and from Preisigke in papyrology, from Goodspeed in early Christian literature (*Index Patristicus* and *Index Apologeticus*). An important lexicon of Patristic Greek being prepared at Oxford is nearing completion.

Among grammatical studies Mayser completed (1934) his excellent grammar of the papyri of the Ptolemaic period, and some beginnings were made by L. R. Palmer in the later documents. Of New Testament grammars revised to take account of the new knowledge the best is Debrunner's revision of Blass (7th ed., 1943; reprinted 1949; Anhang, 1950). Significant new treatments have come also in German from Radermacher (2nd ed., 1925), in French from Abel (1927), in English from Robertson (5th ed., 1931) and Moulton and Howard (see Bibliography). The Septuagint is increasingly recognized as an important monument of Hellenistic Greek in spite of its patent Semitisms, but as yet no comprehensive grammar has been produced. Likewise no over-all grammar of Hellenistic Greek has been attempted, though tentative suggestions have been made toward that end and special studies have appeared in countless monographs and articles.

This research has confirmed the view that biblical Greek cannot be isolated from the Greek language as a whole. Hellenistic Greek, of which it is a part, was a language of great variety and vigor, whose influence was dominant even in Palestine in the first century (see Saul Lieberman, *Greek in Jewish Palestine,* 1942). Attempts to account for the Semitic quality in certain New Testament writings by supposing them to be translations from Semitic documents have not been fully convincing, partly on philological and partly on historical grounds.

Bibliography: Félix Marie Abel, *Grammaire du Grec Biblique,* 1907; Adolf Deissmann, *Light from the Ancient East,* tr. from the 4th German ed. by L. R. M. Strachan, 1927; Albert Debrunner, *Friedrich Blass' Grammatik des neutestamentlichen Griechisch,* 8th ed., 1949; Camden McCormack Cobern, *The New Archaeological Discoveries and Their Bearing upon the New Testament,* 5th ed., 1921; Robert Helbing, *Die Kasussyntax der Verba bei der Septuaginta,* 1928; James Hope Moulton and Wilbert Francis Howard, *A Grammar of New Testament Greek:* Vol. I, *Prolegomena,* 3rd ed., 1908, revised German edition, 1911; Vol. II, *Accidence and Word Formation,* 1929; Ludwig Radermacher, *Neutestamentliche Grammatik,* 2nd ed., 1925; Archibald Thomas Robertson, *A Grammar of the Greek New Testament in the Light of Historical Research,* 5th ed., 1931; Henry St. John Thackeray, *A Grammar of the Old Testament in Greek:* Vol. I, *Introduction, Orthography and Accidence,* 1909.

[Sup.] Allen Wikgren.

C

LEXICONS: I. Lexicons of the Old Testament: For more than a century scholars followed the pattern in Hebrew lexicography set by Wilhelm Gesenius (1786–1842). On the basis of his monumental work Francis Brown, with the co-operation of S. R. Driver and C. A. Briggs, issued *A Hebrew and English Lexicon of the Old Testament* (1907). Although long since out of date, this work is still widely used. The most modern edition is *Wilhelm Gesenius' hebraeisches und aramaeisches Handwoerterbuch des Alten Testaments,* prepared by F. Buhl with the aid of H. Zimmern, W. Max Mueller and O. Weber (17th ed., 1915; reprinted, 1949). Long in process of publication have been two new dictionaries: *Lexicon Hebraicum et Aramaicum Veteris Testamenti* (1940–), edited by F. Zorell and T. Semkowski; and *Lexicon in Veteris Testamenti Libros,* edited by L. Koehler and W. Baumgartner. The latter, which supplies both English and German meanings, appeared from the press in several fascicles (Parts I and II, 1948; III, IV, and V, 1949; VI, VII, and VIII, 1950; IX and X, 1951). The complete text is now available in two volumes (1951–54).

Related to developments in Hebrew lexicography have been certain modern grammatical studies, including: H. Baur and P. Leander, *Historische Grammatik der hebraeischen Sprache des Alten Testaments* (1922), and *Kurzgefasste biblisch-aramaeische Grammatik mit Texten und Glossar* (1929); G. Bergstraesser, *Hebraeische Grammatik* (29th ed. of Gesenius, 1918–29); C. H. Gordon, *Ugaritic Grammar* (1940) and *Ugaritic Handbook* (1947); Z. S. Harris, *Grammar of the Phoenician Language* (1936) and *Development of the Canaanite Dialects* (1939). A real aid to the study of the Greek Bible is the *Theologisches Woerterbuch zum Neuen Testament* (1933–), edited by G. Kittel *et al.* New sources of knowledge of Hebrew, Aramaic, and related languages have called forth numerous special lexical studies.

ELMER E. FLACK.

II. Lexicons of the Greek New Testament: A. ANCIENT GREEK LEXICOGRAPHY: The great Alexandrian scholar, Aristophanes of Byzantium (late third, early second century B.C.), found it necessary to write a work entitled *Lexeis,* in which he explained certain terms in Greek literature which were unfamiliar to people of his time. He was followed by a host of other lexicographers, whose work is now preserved for us to a degree in the lexicons of Hesychius (fifth century A.D.), Photius (ninth century), Suidas (tenth century), and others. As the need arose for Greeks to learn Latin, it was met in the third to fifth centuries of our era by the publication of *Hermeneumata* (in Latin, *Interpretamenta*) which contained an alphabetically arranged Greek-Latin glossary, together with other helps.

B. THE FIRST NEW TESTAMENT GREEK LEXICONS: The New Testament volume of the Complutensian Polyglot (printed 1514, published 1522; New Testament in Greek and Latin in parallel columns on the same page) contained two devices by which a tyro could learn some Greek. The Greek and Latin words corresponding to each other were marked with the same letter of the Latin alphabet, placed slightly above the word. More important, after the Apocalypse there was a Greek-Latin glossary to the New Testament, Ecclesiasticus, and the Wisdom of Solomon; it covered seventy-five unnumbered pages, three columns to a page, and included many inflectional forms in regular alphabetical order. Many words were omitted, and some were wrongly defined, but this meager glossary was the first in a long line of New Testament Greek lexicons.

A concordance of the Greek New Testament is an obvious aid to lexicon-making; the first one was published by Xistus Betulejus (Sixtus Birken) at Basel in 1546. The first separate dictionary containing New Testament Greek words was the *Lexicon Novi Testamenti et ex parte Veteris* of Johann Lithocomus (Cologne, 1552). A work of considerable lexical importance is the *Pars Prima* of the *Clavis Sanctae Scripturae* by Matthias Flacius Illyricus, a Lutheran theologian; it was first published at Basel in 1567. This was a lexicon of both testaments without the Apocrypha, with the word to be defined given in Latin translation; the original Greek or Hebrew word is added for about half of them. The first lexicon of the Greek New Testament alone was Eilhard Lubins's *Clavis Novi Testamenti, seu breve omnium dictionum quibus conscriptum est Lexicon,* a small work which was published at Rostock in 1614.

C. PASOR TO THAYER: In the early period, progress was delayed for a time by uncertainty as to whether Hebrew, the Septuagint, or secular Greek was the most important for interpreting the New Testament. A real advance was made by the appearance in 1619 of Georg Pasor's *Lexicon graeco-latinum in N. T.* at Herborn in Nassau; this was the first dictionary of the Greek New Testament in anything like the modern sense. Its arrangement was largely etymological, i.e., words coming from the same root were grouped together, but it had an alphabetic index that enabled the reader to locate any Greek word. No other New Testament lexicon has gone through so many editions (at least thirty-five in three forms: octavo, manual, and syllabus; revised by Christian Schoettgen, 1716 and 1735, and by Johann Friedrich Fischer, 1774). Its popularity was due to its convenience, clearness, and interconfessional neutrality. Among its faults was a tendency to derive Greek words wholesale from Hebrew and Aramaic, in line with the conviction that Hebrew was the original language of mankind. So, e.g., it derives *kephalē* "head," from Hebrew *kāphal,* "doubled," because the head has two eyes, two ears, and two nostrils.

The next three centuries saw much activity in this field. The *Dictionarium Novi Testamenti* of Ludovicus Lucius (Ludwig Lutz), published at Basel in 1640, was strictly alphabetic in arrangement. There is not a Hebrew word in the book, and it omits prepositions and conjunctions, but it has the virtue of citing every passage in which each word occurs, including the tense-forms of the verbs; it can be used as a concordance.

Among the common faults of this period were neglect of the particles, the inclusion of too few or too many meanings, lack of logical arrangement, and insufficient attention to the Septuagint, secular Greek, and Hebrew. They were gradually being overcome in such Greek-Latin lexicons as those by Christian Stock (1725) and C. Schoettgen (1746). Some of these errors were ably dealt with by Johann Friedrich Fischer in his *Prolusiones de vitiis lexicorum Novi Testamenti* (Leipzig, 1791), a series of thirty-three lectures on the mistakes in New Testament lexicons (arranged under thirty heads), which greatly influenced all good New Testament dictionaries published after its time. Fischer reserved some of his severest strictures for the poor Latinity shown in some of the works.

A modern European language made its appearance in this field first with the publication of *Critica Sacra, or Philologicall Observations upon all the Greek Words of the New Testament, in Order Alphabeticall,* by Edward Leigh (1639+). Leigh, a Puritan and a colonel in Cromwell's army, derived his material from English and Continental scholars of every confession. Although most of his explanations were in English, he distrusted his native language for scholarly purposes, and often gave Latin meanings, even for such simple words as "lamb" and "bread."

Leigh says in the Epistle Dedicatory of his work: "I did desire at the first, to have translated the Greek word by some proper English one; but finding it many times very copious, and of various significations in Scripture, and also our English tongue not so fit as the Latine to render it by, I chose rather . . . to render the Greek word in Latine, and to expresse likewise the word in English, when a fit one was offered, than by tying my self still to the English, to have hazzarded the misinterpreting of the Originall." Leigh's book was later translated into Latin.

John Parkhurst made a Greek-English lexicon, useful but undistinguished, in 1769. Greek-German dictionaries, mostly small and intended for beginners, began to appear with the *Griechisch-Deutsch Lexikon* of Jeremias Felbinger (1657). Others were by Johann Gustav Herrmann (Frankfurt a. d. Oder, 1781) and Eucharius Oertel (Goettingen, 1799).

The influence of J. F. Fischer was shown in the Greek-Latin lexicon produced by his pupil, Johann Friedrich Schleusner (Leipzig, 1792); the later editions of Schleusner contain a list of New Testament Greek lexicons. Further advances were made in similar works by Christian Abraham Wahl (Leipzig, 1822) and K. Gottlieb Bretschneider (Leipzig, 1824).

Wahl's first edition was translated into English (with additions) by the eminent American biblical scholar and archaeologist, Edward Robinson (Andover, 1825). In 1836, Robinson brought out in Boston his own Greek-English lexicon, published in London and Edinburgh the next year. Various revisions brought the book well into the latter part of the nineteenth century. It deserved the high praise given it on both sides of the Atlantic.

The Greek-Latin *Clavis* of Christian Gottlob Wilke (Dresden and Leipzig, 1841) was rewritten and greatly improved by Carl Ludwig Willibald Grimm (Leipzig, 1868). Among the improvements made by Grimm was the inclusion for the first time of many variant readings.

Arrangements were made for an English translation of this valuable work as early as 1864, before it was finished. The translator was Joseph Henry Thayer, then professor in the theological seminary at Andover, Massachusetts. Before he finished his translation a second edition of Grimm appeared in 1879, and this was used by Thayer for his work which was published in 1886 in New York and Edinburgh, when he was professor at Harvard University. Thayer made a relatively large number of changes and additions, which he indicated by enclosing them in square brackets. A corrected edition came out in 1889. This work has served English-speaking scholarship extremely well, though it had the misfortune to appear just before the newer evidence from papyri and inscriptions became available (see Hellenistic Greek).

D. The Twentieth Century: The first important New Testament lexicon after the epoch-making papyrus discoveries of *ca.* 1890 was Erwin Preuschen's *Vollstaendiges Griechisch-Deutsches Handwoerterbuch zu den Schriften des Neuen Testaments und der uebrigen urchristlichen Literatur* (1910). This book met and merited some criticism for not taking full advantage of the newer material. Nevertheless it broke new ground by using German rather than Latin for the first time in a dictionary intended for serious scholarly use, and above all by including the words found in the Apostolic Fathers.

Upon Preuschen's death in 1920 the revision of this book was entrusted to Walter Bauer of Goettingen. When his work was published at Giessen in 1928, it was no longer a *Handwoerterbuch;* the changes and additions which Bauer had made met with universal approval. In 1937 he published in Berlin a third and much improved edition under his own name alone. During the following years Bauer applied himself to the systematic reading of Greek literature from the fourth century B.C. to Byzantine times, and gathered a great number of new parallels to New Testament Greek from it. These he incorporated into a fourth revised edition, which began to appear late in 1949, and came out as a whole in the fall of 1952.

In this magnificent work the words of the New Testament and early Christian literature are more fully illustrated than ever before from the Septuagint, the Semitic background, and especially from the vast body of post-classical Greek literature. The treatment of the prepositions and other particles has been systematized to a degree never before achieved, and there are full references to recent modern literature. An English translation of this fourth edition is now being made by William F. Arndt and the undersigned.

Mention should be made of the useful *Novi Testamenti lexicon Graecum* by F. Zorell (Paris, 1911; rev., 1931), which gives both the meanings and the explanations in Latin.

In the English-speaking world the new evidence from the papyri was utilized in A. Souter's pocket lexicon (Oxford, 1916) and G. Abbott-Smith's manual lexicon (Edinburgh and London, 1921; third ed., 1937). The most important source in the field is James Hope Moulton's and George Milligan's *Vocabulary of the Greek New Testament, Illustrated from the Papyri and other Non-Literary Sources* (1914–29). The ninth revised edition of Liddell and Scott's general lexicon, by H. S. Jones and R. McKenzie (Oxford, 1925–40) has much valuable material for the New Testament.

The *Theologisches Woerterbuch* of H. Cremer (1866; often revised) is once more being extensively revised (since 1933 ed. by Gerhard Kittel, who died in 1948; succeeded by Gerhard Friedrich). Four large volumes have already appeared; the fifth is expected to be finished in 1953, and the last two by 1960. This work deals only with those words that have theological importance, but it treats them much more exhaustively than any smaller work can do.

Bibliography: C. L. W. Grimm, "Kritisch-geschichtliche Uebersicht der neutestamentlichen Verballexika," in *Theologische Studien und Kritiken,* XLVIII (1875), 479–515; E. Mangenot, "Dictionnaires de la Bible," in F. Vigoroux, *Dictionnaire de la Bible,* II (1912), cols. 1419–22; A. Deissmann, *Light from the Ancient East* (Strachan, tr.) (1927), pp. 401–409; F. W. Gingrich, in *Journal of Religion,* Vol. XXV (1945), pp. 179-182; Harold and Blenda Riesenfeld, *Repertorium Lexicographicum Graecum; a Catalogue of Indexes and Dictionaries to Greek Authors* (*Coniectanea Neotestamentica,* XIV), 1953 [New Testament Lexicons, pp. 29–35].

F. Wilbur Gingrich.